Turbulence
in the
River

Aatnan's Four Lessons and Two Truths

Turbulence

in the
River

Restoring
Your Spiritual
Birthright

Michael Sawaya

Editing: The Book Shepherds, Judith Briles & Katherine Carol
        Editing by John, John Maling
        Munson Communications Editorial Services
Cover Design: NZGraphics, Nick Zelinger
Interior Design: WESType Publishing Services, Inc., Ronnie Moore

ISBN 978-0-615-28714-0
LCCN: 2009-925564

10 9 8 7 6 5 4 3 2 1

1. Body, Mind, Spirit   2. Self-help

Printed in Canada

The Observant Press
1600 Ogden Street
Denver, Colorado 80218
www.ObservantPress.com

Dedicated to the human spirit that strives
to find its most perfect place and its ultimate
enlightenment by the path within.

Even your body knows its heritage and its rightful need and will not be deceived

And your body is the harp of your soul,

And it is yours to bring forth sweet music from it or confused sounds.

And now you ask in your heart, "How shall we distinguish that which is good in pleasure from that which is not good?"

Go to your fields and your gardens, and you shall learn that it is the pleasure of the bee to gather honey of the flower,

But it is also the pleasure of the flower to yield its honey to the bee.

For to the bee a flower is a fountain of life,

And to the flower a bee is a messenger of love,

And to both, bee and flower, the giving and the receiving of pleasure is a need and an ecstasy.

—Kahlil Gibran, *The Prophet*

Contents

Contents

Acknowledgments

My deepest gratitude is to the Love, the Creator, whose great support of life and interest in life was central to the teachings of the spirit Aatnan. Aatnan would have me say that he is deep in my Realm of Gratitude and if you read this book you will see what he means. I am grateful that my awareness was opened to the tremendous resources that living in Gratitude brings.

I am grateful to Aatnan for giving me the Four Lessons and Two Truths that you will read about in this book. Being truly grateful in the lessons of Aatnan means living to the full extent of your capabilities and the resources made available in this life. That means taking a lifetime to be grateful. I am relaxed in my awareness and ready to experience more as Aatnan would have you and me do with each of our days on this Earth.

The best gratitude is in living each day to the fullest and giving one's intentions and desires to the creator. Giving one's full intentions and desires does not deplete anything. It only serves to fill the great well that is the core of each of us. I acknowledge this challenge. I am grateful to the spirit that I can pass this message on.

I am also deeply grateful for the brave souls that have so often written about the human potential that lies outside of what was conventional wisdom of the day. The small limb that I have climbed out on in writing this is nothing compared to the efforts of those intrepid early writers—Henri Bergson, Teilhard de Chardin, Thomas Merton and so many others—who have helped to open our human potential and our human spirituality.

Author's Note

f you have questions or thoughts about the teachings and lessons, please don't hesitate to contact me through the *Turbulence in the River* website and its blog:

www.TurbulenceInTheRiver.com

Frequent postings are made and I would be delighted to expand on what he has told me to help you understand and apply it in your lives. Most of all, I hope that you can use these teachings to find your own spiritual and worldly growth. Nothing would please me more, and I know nothing would please Aatnan more.

—Michael Sawaya

Introduction

One ordinary day in July 2003, while flying from Denver to Grand Rapids, Michigan, to attend a wedding, something very extraordinary happened to me. I had recently read a fascinating article in *Scientific American* about parallel universes. During the flight, and being in a contemplative mood, I thought it might be interesting to meditate and try to "step to the side" of myself and somehow influence the universe.

My mediation took me to another realm. In my mind's eye, I thought that I might be to the left of my physical self. Instead, I felt I was not alone. A voice surfaced in my head saying,

You don't belong here.

It then said that I should go back to my normal place and let him help me if that was what I wanted. What did that mean? Normal place? Who was this voice?

Such an experience was entirely new to me. I had been practicing law for 28 years. Certainly, I had never conversed with a Spirit before. That was to change—this Spirit and I conversed on and off for four years. We talked of many things. When I began asking him specific questions about spirituality though, he said he was not into teaching and he introduced me to another Spirit who was a teacher. The teacher was a patient Spirit named Aatnan (pronounced aht-nahn). He gave me the lessons and truths contained in this book. Aatnan opened up for me a new understanding of my world, my feelings toward others, and my integrity as a person. I also learned a new way of understanding and connecting with our Creator, whom Aatnan simply called "Love."

In one of our conversations, Aatnan told me,

It is your birthright to enjoy your world. It is your birthright to savor the world around you and to know the resources that are at your command. It is your birthright to be connected to all of Life and to know and receive the power and attention of Love.

Revelation of the Truths

Aatnan spoke often of Two Truths that are transcendent and fundamental bases of existence. The first Truth is *Love*. Love is the primal force, the Creator of all that is. The second Truth is *Wisdom*. Wisdom sets the rules for the processes of the physical world. Our world and the universes are understood through the Two Truths. You and I live with them and through them. The Truths explain our flesh and bones and how and why our universes were born and are perpetuated.

Many times Aatnan said that understanding the truth of Love is vital for us to achieve spiritual advancement. He was very insistent as he counseled me on this point. His charge to me was to tell anyone and everyone how important it is to know that Love, the Creator, is keenly and intently concerned with who we are, what we think and what we desire.

Being authentic was paramount in all our conversations. The Lessons of *Gratitude, Calmness, Compassion* and *Inclusion* were revealed. In them, you will learn how to achieve both personal and spiritual advancement. These powerful Lessons will ground you in your physical world, engage your mind and open your heart and all parts of your feeling self, as you partake in the fullest experience of the physical world.

Aatnan often expressed the wish that his words would help each seeking person find a path to true fulfillment. His clear messages were for the advancement of all; not the elite or the select few. If you have the intent and desire, you can learn to tap into the infinite source of the great Creator and be taken to the heart of both your person and your spirit.

Share the Message

Early into our initial conversations, Aatnan asked me to write down his words on the Lessons and the Truths. I agreed to do so. After I spent some time reflecting on and delving into the first lesson— the Lesson of Gratitude—he presented me with another challenge. He wanted me to use "my words" and "my voice" as he relayed his insights to you, the reader.

At first, I didn't feel I was up to the mission. I was reluctant to be his messenger. My words, my voice, were those of a litigator—I spent long hours each day challenging and defending the Davids against the Goliaths. And then Aatnan said,

Who better than you?

Aatnan left me a tremendous gift. Through his Lessons, my life, my spirit, opened up even more… and my thoughts became clearer. Because of Aatnan, my life has become truly meaningful and authentic.

As you progress through *Turbulence in the River*, you find that Aatnan's words are in italics and off-set within the text so that they are distinguished from mine. You will find that the Lessons are process-oriented; most likely, you will find that changes will come to you quickly.

A careful reading is recommended—each sentence adds a dimension worth pondering over. Some of his words have a different meaning than you might ordinarily have for them. The terms *gratitude, compassion* and *thought* go far beyond Webster's definitions.

For reference, I have included a glossary of Aatnan's terms with explanations at the back of the book that you will find helpful. Aatnan's concern was that we be given a practical process to stay on a spiritual growth path.

Revealing the Paths

In your search for Enlightenment, you will discover many paths. The Four Lessons and Two Truths from Aatnan are certainly not the only spiritual path.

Humans lead a complicated and fast-moving life. That, together with their general lack of spiritual training, has resulted in too many not being able to achieve spiritual advancement.

Little did I know that when I first heard from Aatnan, how much I would grow. His words changed my view of myself, my view of spirituality, even my world-view. His charge to me was to share and present his words to others. It was no longer a "charge," it was a new focus—a passion to get them out.

While I had never known a Spirit, I'd had some experience in spirituality. Several decades ago, my mind was opened to the immense opportunities for human growth and the expansion of life through the writings of Henri Bergson and Teilhard de Chardin. My explorations continued through the writings of the Sufis, of Thomas Merton, the New Testament of the Holy Bible in its Greek version (which I painstakingly translated over long study!), and many, many other writings in religious traditions, including Christianity, Buddhism and Hinduism. The writings of the ancient Chinese, as translated in the *I Ching* and others, gave me a sense of the depth of the human character and society.

I know now that all of these great writers and great traditions prepared me to be ready to listen for those voices that lead to deeper understanding of the spirit that guides us all. Without these writers, I certainly would not have felt as secure in connecting with a spiritual voice and transcribing the words that came to me.

And so it is with the most eager, but humble, anticipation that I present *Turbulence in the River: Restoring Your Spiritual Birthright.* It is my hope that this book is useful in bringing you an understanding of yourself; that it reveals how you fit into the great universes and connects you to the great Creator.

Looking back, I am now not surprised that Aatnan's voice came to me. I was ready.

It is my sincere wish that you claim your birthright and unfold all that can be.

—Michael G. Sawaya

Conversations
with a Spirit

 ow does one actually converse with Spirit?

Certainly nothing could have prepared me for that day on the plane when I had my first encounter with one. The Spirit's voice was not something I heard with my ears, but rather something I clearly recognized as a conversation in my mind with a voice that was not mine. I remember thinking, "Oh my, that's not my voice talking." I am good at talking to myself and I'm good at talking for others; and, I know the difference.

Aatnan's voice was different than the other Spirit's. Interestingly, Aatnan's voice always came to me from what seemed to be the left side of my head. With a low voice that spoke slowly and very deliberately, his tone and manner were exceedingly kind and generous. I never felt lectured to, even though I had so many questions. Aatnan spoke in a way that made me think my questions were important. His words and ideas were always presented in a methodical, calm and very serious manner. My way of speaking to myself in self-talk is frequently humorous; his was devoid of any.

Occasionally I would get a message from him without having first made a request; but most all his messages came after I presented him with specific questions. To set the stage for our dialogue, I would have to clear my head of other issues and then ask the questions, sometimes several times, before he would begin to answer.

To ask those questions I had to be in a mild meditative state. Typically it was late at night when my wife and young daughter had gone to sleep. Concentration was important. Lights were low, a simple quartz crystal was held in my hand. I quieted my breath, cleared my mind and welcomed the universe.

When Aatnan gave an answer, it usually came in a slow but steady stream. Immediately, I would write down what he told me on a legal pad, my pen scratching out his words or dictating them into a small tape recorder I kept by my side. As each session ended, I looked forward to the next. As his messages unfolded, I knew I would always come away with something I could never have thought up on my own.

After four years, Aatnan left. At first, I felt deserted. He had become almost a confidant and a treasured advisor. And he was gone. His charge to me: spread the word, share my message.

I had not realized how dedicated I would feel bringing his ideas to the world. As I compiled his words, shaping them into what you have in your hands, I'm certain that he will be pleased that anyone would read the generous Lessons he gave to me.

PART ONE

The Lesson of Gratitude

Divine we are,
Gratitude would
have itself known,
by its own,
As part of and
Mirror to
The ultimate knowing
Of our divine Creator.

In the Beginning

Aatnan said,

Gratitude is the beginning of the road to understanding and accessing the spirit. As with any road from here to there, getting to the goal of spiritual development requires starting at the beginning.

These words started the lessons he would share with me that would ultimately change my life. "Why is Gratitude the beginning?" I asked.

Aatnan replied,

Because it is the opening of the access to the world outside the body. It is actually the reconnecting of the spirit to that which it is intimately and ultimately bound.

Gratitude is the energy that overcomes all other energies it comes in contact with. It is like a sound that drowns out all others. It does not seek to control or to influence. It can embrace.

It can meekly make its presence known, but it does not seek to direct anything. It is like the child in the father's arms and it is like the child at its mother's breast. It opens one kindly to the world.

Gratitude stills the mind, because true Gratitude does not allow thoughts except those that complement the gentle and accepting spirit which only seeks to absorb and reflect.

How does this come about? What allows one to reach the place where Gratitude can comfortably rest?

Gratitude requires taking away the "I" and the "It." It requires opening the middle part of one's self where there is only the feeling of open warmth and connection with that which has allowed one to be, to grow, to thrive, to enjoy. It is the opening to the All that has created the vast universe in which we are both the invisible

16

speck and the very vast complexity of the universe itself.

The "Gratitude" that this lesson would have you learn is not the "thanks" for a specific thing received. Rather it is an open feeling of warm embrace and ratification of all the supporting substance that we encounter and which surrounds us. With the most benign energy, Gratitude opens that part of one where the energy of the Being both projects and connects. The place, in the physical body, where that connects is the heart.

Practice the attitude of Gratitude. Allow it for a second, for a minute, for twenty minutes. Make it a comfortable response. Take a bit of it into each moment, and make it the space between each thought. It will become a habit.

Take all that is good and all that is supporting and put it around you to facilitate the open feeling of warm embrace that is Gratitude, but do not seek to win those resources in your Gratitude. Rather, know that those resources and supporting things are yours in abundance, many more than you know or can ever hold or count. The help that is needed in any given situation will be given without asking for it. The Love that one needs is all around, in abundance beyond conception.

Gratitude allows the human heart to open as large as it possibly can. It truly opens the heart to allow it to emit and connect at the greatest levels possible. If there is a feeling of inadequacy, Gratitude will banish that feeling to the place in the body where it can live alone and wither. If there is a feeling of superiority, that feeling, too, is put away where issues of the ego go when they are no longer necessary to serve as the props for a failing Self. When there are thoughts of the judgment of relationship, good or bad, those thoughts are sent back to the mind to be used later when grading or judging may have some temporal value. Gratitude does not need them.

Gratitude is content to encounter the universe. No matter what happens, with Gratitude one knows that all is okay in the connection with the universe. Gratitude is not everything, but it is the road to learning all, and is the beginning of the opening that leads to the realization of oneness and unlimited being.

Living in the Realm of Gratitude requires living in the "is" of Now. The "is" takes in all the past and future. The nuances of experience are what change both the past and the future. The past is changed in its effect on the "is" of Now, when we change the nuances of Now, and likewise the future is changed when we change the nuances of what we expect, see, and feel about the future. Practicing living in the "is" of Now will serve to expand your feeling of Now.

Gratitude, Process, and State of Being

 ater Aatnan told me,

Gratitude is a state of being. It is also a process. In its state of being, it has a set of attitudes that leads one to being open to as many variations and styles as possible. The state of being allows always for a sense of awe that the possibilities available from the resources of the universe are endless.

Its state of being requires a sense of removal from the variations of emotional entanglement and attachment that inevitably cloud one's judgment. Nearly all the emotional states—for

*example, pride, fear, and embarrassment—
cloud one's vision and judgment.*

*The state of being of Gratitude requires that one
take a perspective that is removed from
judgment as to the relative worth or quality of
one's self or others. It requires removal from the
emotional attachments or entanglements that
tend to paralyze a candid or unbiased view of
the realities and the opportunities of any
situation.*

*Gratitude requires being removed from
judgment and emotion because one cannot be
open to as many of the universe's resources as
possible if the five senses and the more subtle
ones of the heart and intuition serve to limit in
any way.*

*One is limited in outlook by the language one
uses and by the manner in which one is
educated. Achievement of a perspective of
removal from judgment and emotion will
always be relative. The act of moving in that
direction allows for Gratitude. True Gratitude
is an ideal, the achievement of which is most
likely rare indeed.*

Be dispassionate and detached in your view of resources. Realize that there are infinite resources and infinite uses for resources. Develop a dynamic relationship toward resources. Always be open and aware of what is around you.

You cannot achieve a solution to a problem situation without a sense of detachment from the situation. Without Gratitude you cannot solve problems. This is true of problems of doing and problems of making. All these dynamic processes of creativity require always looking at your resources with a new view. Try to stay away from attitudes that keep you connected always to how you have done things before. Be aware of the blessings you have received from your world. Also be open to the new that comes to you from the infinite.

3

Gratitude and
a Connection
with the Infinite

Be comfortable in your connection with
the infinite, and with the divine
Creator. Be comforted by it. The practice of
Gratitude will allow an ease of connection to
your Creator. The feeling of connection with the
divine Creator is itself an act of Gratitude. You
live in a world of material things, and you have
many connections with humans and other
living beings. There is much that is evidence of
the creation of the divine Creator. Through
those things and those connections you may
perceive the divine Creator. Your act of
connection to the divine Creator need not take

*you away from your connection to the physical
Realm of Gratitude. Both connections are an
act of Gratitude.*

A rush of new questions poured forth. I asked
him about feelings of depression, of being uncon-
nected, unappreciated, inadequate and unable to
express one's feelings to another. How would the
Lesson of Gratitude address these common feelings
that so many of us experience?

In response, I received this answer:

*When one allows the full access of the resources
and the blessings of life, the feelings of
inadequacy and lack diminish or disappear.
Depression happens when your view of your
internal resources as well as the external
resources is obscured or cut off. Depression is a
strong counteracting force to Gratitude.*

*You have been taught that even in the state of
plenty you must always be aware of inadequacy.
This is a strong force in opposition to your being
able to enjoy the many blessings that have come
your way. This serves to neutralize Gratitude,
and it actually obscures the view that you have
of your resources and your opportunities.*

I then asked Aatnan how I could be in Gratitude when many of those around me so obviously do not understand Gratitude, nor assess its resources.

The state of development of those around you has nothing to do with your own sense of Gratitude. Concentrate on your own state, your own resources. Leave the state of the other to his or her own consideration. Concentrating on their issues and seeing their inadequacies only obscures your own view of the world around you. It is counterproductive to the practice of Gratitude.

Well, then I asked if I had Aatnan's permission to contemplate how these lessons might be applied in the world. He said,

Only through consideration for the effect of lessons on yourself can you have a good view of your own resources. That is the essence of Gratitude. The Lesson is about your own relationship to the universes.

Gratitude requires being directly in the here and the Now, balanced equally between the past and the future. From the past there are so many

resources upon which to draw: common and shared reality to interpret the universes, relationships, material possessions, and so much more. From the future that draws you, there are infinite possibilities. The future embraces you with the richness of resources, known and unknown. It gives you a sense of becoming.

With Gratitude, the past and the future provide the moment of the present with a type of leverage that allows each perceived individual fact of reality, past and future, to be lifted into not only a place of importance but also into a fullness that supports and energizes the sense of being that you know of as your existence. The present is only the briefest moment in time. It is the continuity of the past to the future. It is through Gratitude that the present moment becomes full and weighty.

You must know that Gratitude requires the suspension of judgment. It requires acuity of sense perception. It requires awareness. It also requires the acknowledgment of genius in yourself and in others.

4

The Now

Pondering on what Aatnan had just shared, I asked him for an exercise or a practice that might allow me to fully concentrate on the resources available within the Realm of Gratitude.

He instructed me to sit in a position that would be best for a quiet meditation and let myself be completely in the present moment of Now. He cautioned me to avoid letting the past interfere and to not feel any attachment or attraction to the future.

I was told to visualize that the past can be comfortable in the present, free of disorder and with more than adequate protection for all my memories and lessons of the past.

He assured me not to worry about the future pressing in, nor to worry about it drifting too far away. He encouraged me to let the future be where I could find it quickly, if I needed it.

Sitting in quiet meditation, concentrating on the present moment of Now, I felt a pull and a swell of energy in the area of my heart chakra. I let the energy feeling in my heart grow. I realized that what I was feeling was not a single point of energy, but was like a flow of energy. This was the river of energy—a River of Nows—that Aatnan revealed.

The moments of Now are infinitely small and are gone long before their presence can be felt.

The moments of Now become a River that enters into the physical Realm, the Realm of Gratitude. Everything in the Realm of Gratitude comes from the instant moment of Now.

I was told to go to a place that I might think is located before the source of the River of Nows. He said that I could not get to that place, but that by trying to go there, I would get as close as possible to the place of the origin of the River where the moments of Now begin.

Doing as he said, I felt an immediate rush of energy, something that electrified me from my toes to the top of my head as I tried to reach a place before the start of the River Aatnan told me about.

This is the place where the Creator is bringing all the infinite resources of the universes to be available to connect to your River.

Concentrating my meditation on that place, he added, would allow me to feel the great expansion and the tremendous opportunities available in the Realm of Gratitude. Holding that space open with frequency and regularity would allow me to access the resources of the Realm of Gratitude. My energy would be heightened, inviting new resources that would complement my position in the Realm of Gratitude. This would allow me to continue growing as the universe expands with infinite resources.

Meditation became a regular routine where I could dedicate 30 minutes of uninterrupted time. Sometimes, I would be able to connect quickly with the energizing place close to the start of the River; at other times, it took longer. Each meditation would culminate with my feeling connected to the awesome energy of the moment of Now. There, I felt a sense of great security, knowing that all is possible in the Realm of Gratitude.

In my heart, I felt that Miracles could happen. Deep within me, I felt that there were infinite resources that would only be limited by what my River would allow.

In our early sessions, Aatnan told me that I would understand more as we shared our time together. I remember him saying that we mostly attract only what we already have and that I would learn how to attract things other than what I presently had. He encouraged me to bring my desires into my heart to make them my heart's desire. In doing so, they would invite resources from the moment of Now to fulfill those desires.

The exhilaration of the meditation on the instant moment of Now is both calming and energizing. It always leaves me with a certainty that what we all have in the Realm of Gratitude is what we are going to get. There is always something new, something unforeseen and something incredible.

Everyone's universe shifts when new resources are introduced. These resources are infinite. Aatnan declared that by bringing new resources into our Realm of Gratitude, we are actually shifting our universe. Shifts can be slight, subtle, or significant.

When the magnitude is great, your awareness is heightened and you feel the actual shift.

I looked forward to my meditations with Aatnan. They gave me a deep feeling of security that what I desired would happen.

Later Aatnan would reveal more to me on how and why this meditation works.

5

Finding the Now from the Realm of Gratitude

 *ou can find me in the instant moment of Now.*

Through my conversations with Aatnan, I learned it is not necessary to go there, however, to find connection to the Realm of Gratitude.

Think what this means and why the removal from the instant moment of Now might actually be spiritually important for you.

At first, I thought this removal from the moment of Now was important only because it afforded a different perspective than being in that moment.

Upon deeper reflection, it came to me that being slightly removed from the moment of Now shows that Gratitude is always a process, something for which I must be grateful. It reveals that I truly am a part of the development of the creation of my life. Life is not really about having completed something; it is about becoming. The past is one aspect of becoming, as it is a component of what is happening. The future is another part. Together, they provide the attraction of resources to one's life.

I wanted to know if being in the position slightly before the Now would give me a better place from which to actuate my desires and my requests of the Now. Would it be important in making creations and compelling associations?

Yes. Doing so requires that you have the desire to find the compelling association and fulfilling act of creation from the Now. Even though you are removed from the actual moment of Now, your desire will attract what you need to fulfill those desires.

The spirit of Gratitude is present in you at least from the day of your birth, and will be with you until the day you pass from this physical plane. It is that which serves to energize and excite, to motivate, and to inspire. So often the spirit of Gratitude is used to create nothing and it, in essence, is nothing more than a fleeting feeling of energy or exhilaration, which does not leave a lasting impact.

This you see, for example, in the young man with his foot on the gas pedal feeling the exhilaration of the speed of the car. This young man is using his feelings of Gratitude in what is really a very wasteful way. This young man is over-indulging in the rush of excitement that comes from the power of the moment of Now. Lasting changes and lasting achievement, the kind that may shift one to a new universe, come from being close enough to the moment of Now, and filled with great desire, to communicate one's desire, but not so close that the excitement is overwhelming. You must stay alert and aware to see, recognize, and use the resources that the power of the moment of Now will send to you.

As I contemplated his words, the sense of slight removal seemed to be the operative place to find Gratitude. When you are too close to the emotional and sensory aspects of creation, it can slow down or actually choke off the process of finding Gratitude.

6

Gratitude as a Realm of Both the Past and Future

I asked Aatnan if he would be available to me again. Feeling a bit bold at using my own ideas and inventions to explore the issues of the spirit, I would prefer it if the ideas came directly from him.

Even though you and I are working with lessons that I've presented to you, the spirit is at its core and is the basis for your own experiences. The only way to understand is through experience.

Meaning: What I am able to experience and to present as the spirit, and the spiritual, is indeed *of* the spirit and is indeed spiritual.

Could you give me some guidance as to the validity of my own thinking that we each have the spiritual going on in us at some level, even if we are not aware of it?

Aatnan replied,

Yes, your thinking is correct. Each person is spiritual and all of life involves working with the spirit. Through the practice of spirituality you learn ways to expand and open to the infinite possibilities of the universes. It allows you to pass beyond the closed loops of experience that keep you doing the same things over and over. It allows you to find new and certainly more appropriate ways of interacting with yourself, with others, and with your world.

Does our present affect our past?

I am of the past, so yes it does. What you have as memories of the past are only that: memories. In fact as you make changes and as there are shifts in the way things are done, there are changes in the past, but you will never know how or why. It is not in your experience or your senses to see it. It is far more complicated than you can fully understand.

How do we as humans make changes?

You do it by being what you want changed, not simply by asking for it, or even by trying to make specific things happen. You can only do new things if you are willing to "be" what you want changed. You can see this in the meditation that has been shown to you. Through it you learn how to change the way you experience your daily life. If you would be healthy, for instance, be "health." You will never be truly healthy simply by fine-tuning separate parts of your health. You will do it by the unified state of being health.

I then asked him how long I needed to continue working on the Gratitude exercise before I moved on to the next lesson.

There are a lot of things you need to explore and develop that will provide much more of a basis for spiritual development. The Realm of Gratitude is the basis for all your spiritual achievement. The exploration of the Realm of Gratitude, and the fuller understanding of that Realm, will serve to open you up. It will make you and your resources more available to you in the present. It will provide the basis for you to grow into the spirit. Do not underestimate it. Gratitude is the basis of spirituality.

7

Adversity and the Attitude of Gratitude

atnan told me,

The attitude of Gratitude requires being open to and embracing all of those things and all of those events that happen in your life. It requires suspending judgment to the greatest extent that one can.

Adversity inevitably provides the outline for opportunity. The person condemned to death knows that the walk to the gallows clearly frames what is left of the opportunities of his or her life. A charging, enraged animal provides the frame for escape, which is the only

opportunity that might be provided at that moment.

The adversary in personal or business life also clearly frames the opportunities that are available to the individual or the business. One's adversary or even one's nemesis is a resource to the individual. It is all a matter of perspective, and all events in one's life have limitations in any given moment.

The attitude of Gratitude will not work well for you when negative emotions or judgments are allowed. By judgment, I mean a decision as to the ultimate value of any given event or thing. Everything is relative. The value of any thing or action in any given situation is entirely dependent upon the other things or events that are evident in the situation. Decisions made about the ultimate value of any action or any thing will inevitably block your spiritual development.

For the attitude of Gratitude there are only resources. There are no non-resources. Awareness and discernment will reveal to you how any resource is useful to you when you become aware of it. What you first think is useful may actually be useless to you when you try it. Keep looking and always be aware. What you first think you dislike may actually be what you needed all along.

What is harmful to you in a large amount might, for instance, be exactly what you need in a small amount. For the Realm of Gratitude, experience will be a great teacher.

8

Achievement and Spirituality

The physical grounding of your existence, through the Realm of Gratitude, also provides the grounding of your spiritual existence. Every action that you take in your world is at its core an exercise in creation, involving observation at a high level, and a concentration of Thought that would baffle the wildest imagination.

Spiritual advancement necessarily, and intrinsically, involves becoming increasingly aware of one's self and the world and the living beings with which you interact. When you achieve, when you make something happen by physical and mental activity, you are truly *engaged in something that is a spiritual activity. When you understand this, you can know that everything you do by organized activity is not only special, but partakes of aspects of the divine.*

All of Life is important to the divine. Your human abilities of observation, which allow increased abstraction as well as fine discernment, make you even more important to the divine.

Achieving what you want from the physical world, and all its connections, begins in the Realm of Gratitude with the start of your life and ends at the time of your death. It is an inborn drive that you cannot ignore. Various methods are chosen to satisfy wants. Some do it by guile, some by theft, some by bartering what they already have, some by buying it outright, some by entreaty and some by logical argument.

It is universal that humans seek to achieve.

You advance yourself spiritually, in the achievement of your wants, by the maximum awareness of what your wants are. Understand what you are observing, not just what you want. Try to observe even yourself in the act of searching and achieving your wants. Recognize that the mere desire of your wants is evidence of the great connection that you have with all the cohesion that the great universes have in their deepest nature. This is all created by the divine, and perpetuated by it. You will learn in the spiritual Truth of Love that all the universes are perpetuated by it.

Love is the source of all that is divine.

You may not always understand the why of your wants. That is something only the Truth of Wisdom can fully explain. You should know that some of your most basic wants involve workings of Wisdom far deeper and more complex than even the best and brightest could possibly ever fully understand.

There are some who would advise you to limit your wants to achieve spirituality. They are teaching a path to spirituality that differs from what these lessons will teach you. The Lesson of Gratitude teaches that you do not necessarily need to ease up on your wants, or on the various methods of achieving them. Achievement in the physical world is not proof, by itself, of any spiritual awareness or spiritual achievement. Likewise, great achievement is not evidence of any spiritual limitations.

You see your achievements in the River of Nows. The River is variously clear and murky, still or fast moving. Always it is part of the rushing River that enfolds with the infinite, its source, so quickly that it foils any attempt to know how and why Wisdom created it in the first place. It is certain that even the act of attempting to discern what is available in each instant moment of Now must elude the best developed among the human senses.

I asked Aatnan if one should cease caring where the achievement comes from, or what its worth might be.

Yes to the latter but no to the former. Achievement for the human necessarily involves spiritual process, but not necessarily spirituality or spiritual development. Achievement involves change and change involves dynamic combinations, all of which are born in the cauldron of the Now.

All human achievement, even the satisfying of basic wants, involves accessing the Realm of Gratitude. We are all born into the spirit and all of our lives involve constant Thought, at one level or another. All thought connects us to Love. Through this connection, all of Life adds to the force of Love, and all Life is on a course that may lead to a reunion with Love at some level of Enlightenment.

Awareness and Attention

The beautiful sunset with its many hues and flights of color is a gift to anyone who would take the time to see it. How few are those in a hurried city who give the time to stop and see it? How few are those who stop to see the rose, much less to smell it? How few are those who take the time to hear the notes of the songbird sung without any price of admission?

It is the same with so many of the resources that the universes give so freely. Rushing to compress more resources in ever smaller and tighter places, it becomes less likely that there will be time or energy to be aware and to pay attention to what there is to be enjoyed.

*Yet, the attitude of Gratitude requires
awareness and demands attention be given to
all the resources that the mind, senses, and
intuitions are able to identify.*

*It is the very essence of the attitude of
Gratitude that is the basis of your spirituality.
To be attentive first requires awareness.
Awareness requires the cultivation of the
senses, the quieting and refining of the mind
and the opening of the heart and other centers
of intuition. Awareness is possible only to the
extent that the mind, the senses, and the
intuition are able to detect any specific
resource. Thus, awareness is useful to detect
only the known, not that which has yet to
be identified.*

*This is so obviously true with respect to that
which the eye cannot see, such as the individual
molecules and the atoms of every physical thing.*

*The brave ones, the adventurers, and the genius
pave the way for the rest to find the resources
that their awareness may then bring to their
attention. It is not itself sufficient to tell one to
be brave, to undertake adventures, or to create*

*in the way that the genius does. These acts
require an internal drive, internal energy, and
internal connection that defy description.*

*These acts are versions of Gratitude opening
onto itself. It is the willingness to grasp and
absorb resources in their raw form without
preconception as to the meaning or the form. It
is the willingness to encounter, see, and feel the
resources of the universes in all their macro and
micro grandeur.*

*Seeing and feeling each resource in as pure and
elegant a form as can be seen or felt serves to
define your essential humanness, your own
spirit, and your connection to the universe. The
challenge to all who would exercise the attitude
of Gratitude is to allow sufficient concentration
and presence of mind, with intuition, to become
aware of both that which is seen and that with
which one has yet to become aware.*

*The more this is done, the more the spirit
grows, both in its substance and its ability to
grow. The challenge begs for individual
practices that foster this concentration and
presence of mind with intuition.*

Deep breathing into the moment of Now,
creating the space that does not allow
interference of the past or future, and sensing
the Great River of Nows can create enough
space and enough energy to allow for the
concentration and the presence of mind with
intuition to catch at least a glimpse of those
resources rushing through the Great River.

Some of the resources of the Great River move
so quickly that the senses cannot detect them,
and the mind can never understand them.
Some can be felt only in the depths of intuition,
and then only faintly. Yet wondrous are those
resources that provide only the subtlest hint of
their presence in the Great River. Awareness
and attention are all about Gratitude and they
are also all about the cultivation of the attitude
of Gratitude.

10
Breathe for Gratitude and Calmness

When you breathe, breathe with your
body's intelligence that knows
instinctively its connection through Wisdom to
the physical realm—the Realm of Gratitude.

Breath is always the most immediate physical
connection to Gratitude. All begins with it and
depends on it. All living beings connect to
Gratitude through breath, or depend upon
another being to do it.

Living beings are so connected to Gratitude
that breathing is done automatically with no

*need for awareness of breathing. When
breathing is disrupted, or even interrupted, the
connection to the Realm of Gratitude is
correspondingly affected.*

*The most effective connection that brings the
most extensive interaction with Gratitude is
that which uses the breath in its fullest and
calmest state. For this reason, attention to
breath, at least enough to keep it calm, deep,
and full, is essential to the fullest enjoyment
of the Realm of Gratitude. It also leads one
naturally into the second lesson, the Lesson
of Calmness.*

*Deep and calm breathing is essential to
achieving higher and more effective connections
to Gratitude. Those who don't have time to
deeply breathe, or time to be calm, are missing
a great deal of what they can get from their
physical world. Pitifully, they are missing out
on not only the most intensive connection with
Gratitude, but they miss also a good deal of the
actual substance of Gratitude.*

*Far worse, they miss out on their most effective
connection with the instant of Now. They*

thereby miss their most intensive connection with Love, the Creator. They do, further, miss their most effective methods of influencing their universe. They tend to be those to whom events happen. They are not the ones who tend to be the most effective in making things happen.

My own observation on this lesson is that our collective consciousness is probably in many ways preset. Our brains are pre-wired for our physical being and for so many basic emotional states that assist in our preservation and our elementary interaction with the physical world. Our basic view of reality is shaded, if not dictated, as linguistic creatures, by the language we use.

We are, therefore, not completely free at any time to see things in ways fundamentally different from that which we have been taught and by what our language allows us to consider. Our Rivers are in so many ways preset for us before we begin our journey in this life. When we get to the chapters on the Truths of Love and Wisdom, you will find Aatnan's revelations enlightening.

11
Gratitude and the Adventurer

he spirit is not just about you, or any other individual person. It is about relationship. Humans are all about relationship.

You certainly see everything through your two eyes, hear everything from your two ears, feel with your own fingers, and take all the input from your senses to what seems to be an isolated entity. Yet, aside from a few unhappy souls, the billions of humans who have had the good fortune to be born into the physical sphere all have known relationship from the first entrance in the world, if not before.

The spirit is as much about relationship as is all of human society. Spirit is something present between you and your fellow beings. It is something that connects you to the universes. It does not, except in rare circumstances, make itself immediately apparent in the material sphere. It may, and probably always does, express itself in the physical and material sphere, but its true substance lies beyond, between and unseen, much like the air you breathe but cannot see.

There is something else that makes you human, and which explains why you are present in this physical plane, other than what you can see, feel, hear, taste, or smell. This has been known to humans since before anything you have that humans have written. Humans have long known that there are connections between them and the rest of Life and the rest of the universe.

The teachings that I bring to you are not meant in any way to detract from the expressions of the human spirit and expressions of beauty that other teachers of the spirit have produced. Many have shown the connections between humans and the divine. Inspiration can be found in many sources. All lead to the same destination. Always the path that is accessible and inspiring should be the one chosen to walk. Do it for your own sake and not to enrich or support another.

Being in the attitude of Gratitude requires letting go of the ties that bind and the ties that blind. It requires that one let loose, or set loosely, the presuppositions, the biases, the social contracts, the social conventions, and any other limitations on action or thought that would interfere with receiving and enjoying any thing, resource, or energy that is available in the universe at any given moment of Now.

This requires an act of courage or perhaps even a series of lifelong acts of courage to disavow those allegiances into which you have entered that have required a surrendering of your rights to be open to new and different thought, spiritual practice, action, or any other combination of material enjoyment and practice that impact the senses, the heart, and the spirit.

Your neurology, your language, the nature of memory, concepts of time, and even the physical laws of this universe limit your ability to recognize anything you either have not seen before or have not been able to imagine from your assumptions about the physical universe.

However much you try to live only in the moment of Now, you are called back constantly to see the colors you see, taste the flavors you can taste, and enjoy the sensual and material parts of you that we have been preconditioned to know. Thus, the expanse of Gratitude is ever limited no matter how hard you try.

Without the courage to open the senses and open the spirit, you cannot begin to explore the possibilities of the universe in the ever expanding Now. The first seafarers had to have the courage to try out the new idea of floating a far distance in a craft however it may have been first fashioned. Some who tried did not survive. The search for the new has always required courage and fortitude.

Christ was crucified for his new spiritual practice. Many are the new prophets who suffered rejection at the least, and banishment or death at the worst. Churches have punished many who suggested new ideas about the world.

The attitude of Gratitude is not just an attitude of being grateful for what has brought you here. It is about opening the senses, opening the heart, using intuition to the limits of your ability, and doing whatever you can do to know whatever is available in the River of Nows.

The universes are constantly changing, and present possibilities for infinitely great changes. Yet, the process of Wisdom often limits change until it bursts forth in cataclysm, giving rise to a new Order. Understand that change is ever-present and ever limited. Be ready for that, and also know that the Lesson of Gratitude requires that you always be open to change.

Keep your senses aware. Be open and receptive to all that exists. Also be ready to accept the new, the untried and the brilliant genius of new creation. Advanced spiritual growth requires the spirit of the adventurer and the ability to use your senses to know things that others may not have known before.

12

Gratitude and the Heart

 s Gratitude a process of thought alone?

Gratitude is everything you encounter in any given moment. It involves what you bring by way of memory and consequences of the past. It is everything you have in the Now. It is also what is potentially present from the future.

Aatnan reminded me that the past and the future do not exist in the Now. We have only a sense of the past and an anticipation of the future.

Remember that your minds are used to moderate and balance bodily functions. The mind does not exist alone, but it also takes its

cues from the body, and certainly from the
heart. Moreover, the heart does not take orders
from the brain.

When Aatnan taught me how to feel the present
moment of Now, I realized that the place where I
felt the present moment was within my heart
chakra. This is the focus of the energy of the heart.

*The heart passes judgment and gives its input
whether asked or not. It senses the propriety
and sensibility of matters that may contradict,
supersede, or not even involve any specific
process of conscious thought. For this reason,
as well as many others, the input of the heart
cannot be ignored if one is to know how to
relate to and use the myriad of resources
available at any given moment. The heart is
to be cultivated as an integral part of the
interaction with the Now.*

Reflecting on his words, I'm reminded that
certain things, certain actions and certain relations
are asked for by the heart, whether or not the mind
concurs. The best that can be said is that the mind
must be available for messages and input from
the heart. If the mind is closed, the heart may be

constrained to find a method to influence the mind in ways that may be less than cordial.

Gratitude cannot be a process of mental concentration. For the intellectual, this is a challenge. It does find its true expanse in the available benefits that Wisdom has bestowed. It is focused but relaxed, much as the eye is relaxed when concentrating on peripheral vision, rather than on a particular object. It allows as much to come in as it can. It is not looking for any specific thing.

13
Fixated Emotion

he place of Gratitude, Aatnan told me, requires a perspective of the Now. It includes one's self but does not allow for the connection of emotion or a fixation on the thoughts of anything in particular. It requires the ability to be free enough to see as much as possible, and to feel as much as possible, through intuition. Yet, the fixation of thoughts and the emotional states—fear, anger, jealousy, embarrassment and others—has the attribute of controlling the rest of the mind and the heart such that a separation to look at the great plenitude of the unfolding Now may not be possible.

When one is caught in emotion, or fixation of thought, one finds the rest of the unfolding Now to be obscured or blocked off entirely. This is because the only thing, the only thought, and the only state of being allowed is to be in the swirl of the River, fixated by emotion or Thought. How can one even think of getting out of this situation when to do so requires the unfixing of something that is already fixed? Furthermore, emotional states are true chemical states of the body and require time to dissipate even if one is able to start the process to do so.

I asked Aatnan how to allow a cooling of the emotion or a separation from the emotion sufficient to allow for a vantage point and a perspective separate from the unfolding Now.

Gratitude requires awareness of the many aspects of the Now. Your own self, in all its aspects, is, for you, one of the most visible and dominant parts of the infinite Now. Being aware of your own self is essential. You know when you are in the swirl of the River. You can feel when it is pushing and you can feel when it is pulling.

The swirl of the River always makes you feel that you are compelled to act, to protect yourself. Be at least aware when the emotion is beginning to assert its grip. This simple act of awareness requires perspective. This will let you see if you are really in danger and need

*to act in the way that your River is pushing you
to do.*

*The awareness, alone, of the swirling feeling will
diminish the intensity or power of the emotion or
thought. Awareness will allow you to begin to
unfix the emotion and to place it where it will
not be dominant. Be aware of what the emotion
is telling you to do. Be especially aware that you
can wait to follow that emotion when the focused
heart is given time to agree or disagree.*

*Tell yourself that you will do what the emotion
tells you to do if you can have the time to
quietly access your focused heart. Put rocks
around the swirling place in the River to
contain the swirling of the River until you have
time to take it to your heart.*

Later Aatnan would reveal the Truth of Love,
showing how important the heart connection is to
Love. Gratitude is the beginning and the base. It is
the dust and the flesh. It is the joy, the pain, and the
sadness. It is all the relationships that we have and
that we could have.

In the Gratitude Lesson, Aatnan shows how the
swirling pools of the River limit our experience of

the Realm of Gratitude. The Truth of Love shows how the heart connects to Love, the Creator, and accesses those resources necessary to fulfill you.

Aatnan told me many times to always remember that the resources of the Realm of Gratitude are infinite. When one resource appears depleted, turn to another. The mere act of being open brings those resources in abundance.

 The act of being closed, as one is in any of the swirling pools of the River, diverts resources away, creating the appearance of want and deprivation. Acting out in fear, anger, grief or other gripping emotions almost always diverts resources.

When times appear desperate, the spirit would have you open your eyes and ears. It may well be something to answer your need. Or, it may be something to answer a need you have not yet felt.

Always, always remember that the reason for Gratitude is to be aware that what is available to you is much more than you could ever dream.

Go Back from
the Future

Aatnan's response to me was delivered cryptically when I asked if he had any other thoughts on Gratitude:

Go back from the future.

Not knowing what he meant, I assumed that I was to get something from the future and bring it to the present. How I would accomplish it, I did not know.

I meditated further, asking Aatnan for more advice. What did "Go back from the future." mean?

The future has resources just as does the past.
From the past we have memories. From the

future, we have something like the equivalent of memories. The future is infinite in the possible combinations but it will be limited in the manner by which we access it. Likewise, the past appears fixed in its pattern by the manner in which we have accessed the resources of the past.

Aatnan reminded me that the spiritual life and the path of the Lesson of Gratitude require that you look at the future much as you look at the past. The past leaves each of us with memories in the form of sense impressions. Think of the home or apartment of a grandparent, relative or old friend. Your memories of that place may include smells, feelings and visual memories with them that have no direct verbal content. There is a sense of being in the home.

The resources of a possible future event are the same. Each possible future event has companion thoughts, intentions, feelings and energy in the form of increasing vibrations of which we may be at least partially aware. There is as much to the future event as there is in stored-up memories of the past.

Accessing the resources of a possible future event does not necessarily create that possibility. It may, in fact, create it, or something like it, but it may just as well give the necessary resource while allowing for something else in the future. It may be something with more or less of the resources than the possible future event allows.

He asked that I not be overly concerned with one event or another of the past or future. The central theme of the Lesson of Gratitude is that I should be concerned with the here and the Now. That concern should be translated into an attitude of Gratitude. From this attitude actually flows the creation of the possible combination of the here and Now and the future "here and Now." Its purpose is to open our spirit to all that can possibly be. Another way to look at it is that this opening to possibilities also opens you to the spirit.

The attitude of Gratitude is about the opening of the mind, body and heart for each individual in the entire immensity of available resources of any given moment of Now.

The immensity of the resources of the infinite Now is beyond description. It is accessible to us, resource by resource, relationship by relationship and thought by thought. Opening to the immensity of the resources brings a flood of those resources.

Any given moment of Now does not include, as far as our senses can know, anything but a relatively small combination of possible resources. The others exist, just as the thousands upon thousands of items in the grocery store exist, as possibilities, even though one carries home a small number of bags with fifty or less of those items.

As humans, you can, at any given moment of Now, employ only the limited number of resources that are present. You can, however, be open to the infinite variety of resources, known and unknown. The ordinary individual human in the world before electricity probably could never have dreamed what electricity would eventually allow. There were those inventors who, accessing the future and bringing it into the Now, did more than dream of it. They took the human spirit into those resources. The great explorers, the great builders, the great writers, the great thinkers, and those of immense achievement did the same in their time. Watch a small child at play to see the same visionary attitude. All are exploring the possibilities of the resources available in the here and Now.

If you believed only in candles and allowed for no other possible form of light than fire from that source, other possibilities would never come to you. Millions upon millions of human beings lived and died having never been allowed the possibility of anything else. It had not yet been conceived that such resources were available. Those resources were available then, as they are now, but they were not being accessed.

The attitude of Gratitude opens the mind, heart and body to the infinite possibilities in any given moment of Now. It does not allow for limited thinking or for unquestioning adherence to any pattern of feeling or thought. Instead, it requires that the senses be open; that the mind be free to speculate; and that the heart be free to attach or detach as the moment of Now would best allow. It requires that awareness not be limited by anything preconceived.

How do you best access the future resources and "Go back from the future"?

First, realize that any conceivable possibility of the future can be as real as any memory of the past. It should be as real as the first school room of your educational career, and as real as the first amorous kiss.

Undoubtedly the future possibilities include much more than one can conceive. One can know only one's first kiss and not the first kiss of any other of the billions of persons on the Earth. The trick is to be as open as you can be, and sufficiently aware and disciplined, to perceive the combination of the resources that the possible future Now will allow.

I asked him if there were practical processes that could help to facilitate accessing the resources of the future Now. The answer he gave was concise:

Future memories. Live them with every sense re-creation that you do with past memories.

Most of what we see as negative can be expressed in the positive. For instance, you might say, "Touch the stove only when it is cold," rather than, "Don't touch the stove."

The attitude of Gratitude abhors the negative. The negative does not encourage, and, in fact, does not allow for the positive search for all the resources needed for the moment of Now. The positive creates an attitude compatible with the attitude of Gratitude. It is the difference between planting it in hard rock and planting the seed in good soil. Chapter 40, The

Benefits of Using the Negative, provides a further discussion.

Would working with future memories serve to create the actuality of the future memories? I asked him. His answer was,

Yes. The utility of the future memory is more than just conjuring the future into the present, or creating in some future time.

According to Aatnan, the utility is in realizing resources in the present moment of Now. The attitude of Gratitude, being in the Realm of Gratitude, is all about the Now. It allows one to be comfortable and even practiced in the possession and use of resources, in the Now.

Being fully aware is an essential attribute of the attitude of Gratitude. To have a functioning memory of any past event, the full senses as an observer of the past event are essential to the laying down of the completed memory. The same must be true of the future event if it is to have completion.

Aatnan revealed that openness is a necessary part of accessing future memories. Some things can be well appreciated even if they have never been previously experienced, while for many other things it is a great challenge.

Fullness of awareness in the future memory requires the ability to let go of past association and let new ones be established. It also can take great imagination and great intuition.

15
Savoring

Resources come to us both night and day, in all forms of contact with the senses, gratifying our tastes, filling our vision with curiosities and delights with infinite forms, colors, and shapes. They entice our ears, vibrate our energy centers, touch us sensually from vibration to arousal, and envelop us, lifting us, and in so many ways transporting us.

We learn very early the delights of the world of the senses. When it gratifies deeply we may well try it over and over to the extent that it goes from excess to obsession and grabs us with an addiction that we are at a loss to explain.

Filling plates too full, we may forget what it is we are eating, and often drinking so much that the subtlety of taste is lost in the jumble and the flood of its surfeit. Through exuberance of Gratitude, so sure of our attraction to the object of our enjoyment or our consumption, will quickly vanish the very taste we sought, the very jewel of our eyes' delight, the very thing that the resource would give us. The little bit of greed gives us a heavy weight rather than what could have been a beacon or a compass to be used in an act of creation with a resource we love.

The young person does this so stunningly in the drag race down the main street with a rival or a stranger. The motorcycle rider does this in an act of wild abandon that loses contact with the very ease and beauty that the two-wheeled vehicle can give. The glutton does this as King Henry VIII did in taking all that his kingdom could give him, as much and as often as he possibly could. The cooked pork, the veal, the pheasant, the viands of all kinds and the many other tastes become distorted in the wild abandon that the gorging brings.

The very name, the feast, lets us all know that our gustatory tastes may open to the full throttle and race as fast as it can, competing with God-knows-what to accomplish sometimes nothing more than distention and pain. Yet few among the billions of humans would decline the opportunity to stuff to one's delight. The resources of the Realm of Gratitude can stifle rather than energize, and derail rather than give progress to spiritual growth.

Aatnan instructs that the want of savoring is close to the root of all excess and the origin of many obsessions. Savoring is a simple act, requiring only that time be given both during the act of resource enjoyment and for so much time afterward as the vibration and energy of the act continues to keep the sensation of enjoyment that the act allowed.

The taste of the wine or the chocolate or the candy is all the better for the act of concentrating on the place of the taste, the fullness of the taste and the entirety of the feeling that the small gift of resource allows. The vibration of the reciprocating engine of the motorcar is all the more sensational when it is allowed to show the fullness of its strength in a graduation that is observable to the senses. The gift of the animal's meat is truly better when the adequate morsel is taken and savored without hurry or crowding.

The act of human love also becomes something of much more compelling beauty and energy when it is allowed to be taken in slow, deliberate enjoyment, and is ended with a time of holding both the object of its love and the energy it has both taken and given. Savoring. Memory allows for continued savoring and a return to the enjoyment of the resource without a continual wasting of either the resource or the person in the consumption of it.

Aatnan says that concentration on the vibration of the specific resource allows for the enjoyment of both the substance and the beauty of the resource, without the confusion that comes when those vibrations are ignored. In a manner of speaking, each resource has a lesson, and to some extent a medicinal value that is lost when it is not savored in its vibration or vibrations.

The vibration may be the glint the vision gives, or the lift to the tongue or the pallet that the taste provides, or the extra fullness of breath the sensual act or the act of exertion gives. Vibration is found in all the many sensations that remain after the resource is used, observed, or consumed. The meat will lose its savor after a reasonable time, the act of love ends no matter how hard one tries to prolong it, and the wine will absorb into the tongue within a short but sufficient amount of time. Reason and care reveal how long the time of enjoyment should be.

Slow down enough to find the sensation that the resource allows, Aatnan says. Love and Wisdom, being the great truths of spirit, will be better used and enjoyed when their great powers are brought to any situation with a savor and a concentrated purpose of enjoyment. He tells that every emotion, pleasant or unpleasant, resounds deeply into the well of our own being and, to some extent, into the great ocean from which we have come. Spirit has also shown that negative emotions are more often than not a clear sign of what he calls looping behavior. This is behavior that returns to the same place, trying over and over to do the same thing without accomplishing a final satisfactory result. This behavior stops or blocks connection to future resources.

Savoring of resources provides a grounding vibration. In the teachings on the Truth of Love the spirit shows how Love is the foundation force behind all vibration. In the Lesson on Calmness, it will be clear that without a quiet time to gain perspective the River will continue to hold you in its swirling pools. In the teachings on the Truth of Wisdom you will see that savoring is a great ability to learn Wisdom's rules and processes. For the Lesson of Gratitude, savoring is necessary to gain a full exercise of the attitude of Gratitude. That is the grounding for all the lessons and the two truths.

16
Working with Gratitude in Difficult Times

n all lives come difficult times. Some days are filled with the great plenitude of Gratitude awareness. Other days are filled with the confusion that cuts or diminishes awareness of the wealth of resources that Gratitude reveals.

Those difficult times can arise when there are conflicts with someone else; with the elements of nature; with other living beings; with small cells, such as tuberculosis or cancer; or even with viruses that cannot live except within and in conflict with us. When those difficult times arise, they show that the web of Gratitude is not seamless. Gratitude is not one web, but an infinite array of webs inter-connecting in ways that Wisdom only knows. At the very least, it's confounding to us.

Difficulties can cause a disruption of Gratitude awareness. Any difficulty can slow or stop the spiritual growth that Gratitude alone creates. The Spirit teaches that only by use of Gratitude, can discernment flow. Yes, it takes discernment to discriminate. Think of two roses: one yellow, one red. You initially saw the difference between the red and yellow rose—the color discrimination. That was before you demonstrated that you had the ability to trust sufficiently that your senses are able to discern the difference between the colors red and yellow.

Only know that the confusion that comes with difficulty is not a permanent state. The permanent state is not permanent at all, but is a promise of a continuum of revelation of the infinity of the universe created by Love.

Love dispersed itself as it dispersed Wisdom. It is the great promise of Love and the promise of observation that Love is everywhere, supporting all things.

It can be so difficult to hold onto Gratitude when difficulties arise. Recognize when they surface; for they are the turbulence of the River of Nows. This turbulence does not allow one to see clearly what is there. Emotion, pain, hunger or other strong and sometimes overwhelming feelings obscure what resources are close or even directly at hand.

Remember your heart, and feel the great energy of it when difficulties occur. The point of Now is best accessed through the heart; although it is present at other places where energy concentrates within your body. Feel the River of Nows, allowing yourself to get as close as you can to the point of Now.

If you can resist the desire to understand all of the complexity of the River of Nows, you can feel the intensity of the point of Now itself. You may discover there is a vast array of resources, nearly at infinity, that the universe has available for you. This is limited only by your own powers of discernment, and your own timid and somewhat limited ability to observe.

You are part of the River of Nows. In fact, you, and the entire universe, are in Wisdom's plan to hold together the power of Love. The dance of an unfolding creation is known in the embrace of Love and Wisdom.

Aatnan said,

Don't plan to know it all. Don't think that your theories of how, why, and when it all began or where it is going are perfectly correct and on the mark. There will always be exceptions, differing views from differing perspectives, and turbulence caused by the difficulties of life.

Wisdom is too great to have created flaws. What we see as flaws or difficulties is our inability to see clearly and to understand how the infinity of webs fits together. You are blessed that you usually see only one web at a time. You would be overwhelmed if you saw much more than one at a time.

17
Musings on Gratitude

On February 7, 2007, I awoke in the night thinking about the Lesson of Gratitude. I thought how clear it was that so many people fail to bring any real change in their lives. This must be, I thought because their projections for the future are filled with the emotions, feelings, and thoughts that their present looping behaviors have. I concluded that those projections do not create a break from the present.

That same night I dreamed that several levels or types of resources were being laid out, similar to stepping stones, or a block outline form. There were different resources on different levels. One level, which had the most activity and most complicated relationships, apparently was being overseen by a spirit or some entity. The entity said, "These are limitations, and I am giving them to people as lessons to learn."

Upon waking, my thought was that it seemed most of the people who are given these limitations would not escape. Instead, they would be constrained to continue to repeat their lessons.

This dream seemed to come from Aatnan. My interpretation was that we are being led, at least in some ways in our use of the Realm of Gratitude, to learn things about ourselves, and, about how we relate to our universe. I found it useful to consider that problems in my River are not just something to overcome and move beyond, but can teach me about myself and how I am connected to the universe.

So, the attitude of Gratitude would say to the problem, "This is something from which I can learn to better appreciate and better use the resources I have been given." The dream said to me, "Swim with the swirling River, if you can or if you have to, rather than try to swim against it. You might have a better chance of getting out of the turbulence if you do."

Gratitude, and all that comes with it, in the conjuring of material and spiritual combinations, is where the greatest part of the spirit is grasped. But, this is only the first lesson. Beyond it, with Love and Wisdom, are the other lessons that we are required to learn in the search for our own connection to the universe.

PART TWO

The Lesson of Calmness

*From a distant place
the calmness seen.
Below the battle rages.
The guiding hand to
stem the tide
is to the side
or up above.
Be still, be brave,
Your heart to find.*

18
Introduction to Calmness

 asked Aatnan to tell me how to under-
stand Calmness.

Calmness follows Gratitude and is facilitated
by it. The opening of the heart facilitates
Calmness. As the heart opens and when it is
open it allows ease of connection with others in
a manner of understanding that is not hindered
by doubts or other constraints. Calmness
cannot exist without the open heart and it is for
this reason that it follows from Gratitude and
heart opening.

Viewing Gratitude and heart opening from the vantage point of Calmness allows a perspective of Gratitude that is beyond the mere feeling of Gratitude itself. It shows the facility of Gratitude and the value of the human heart in a way that the emoting feeling of Gratitude alone cannot do.

Calmness presupposes connection, as it requires the ability to feel secure both in itself in its relation with others and with one's universe. It is a state of awareness without vigilance, but it requires seeing, feeling, and other sensual awareness to allow its state of aware being. It holds the state of being in a way that knows its relation to others and is comfortable in where it is going, where it has been, and how it is affecting the existence of others around it. Calmness by its very nature requires that there be no desire to harm others, or to cause discomfort that is not internally derived.

Calmness is beyond merely being benign, as it is neutral in what it seeks to cause to both itself and to others. It is in its essence a state of being rooted in a fully aware sensual existence. Calmness in its developed state allows all activities to be more fully experienced, every sound more fully heard, every feeling more fully felt, every sight clearer, and every sound more defined. Mere words cannot convey the depth that you will find in each sensual experience when Calmness is fully present.

Calmness is in part a lesson in balance, as it needs to be free from supports or props to be present. It is more than a state itself. It is partly a quality of existence. It is the taste; it is not the substance. It is the resonance, not the cymbal. It is the savor, not the food. It is not Love, but it allows Love to be present. Calmness allows the knowledge that both precedes words and transcends words. It is therefore essential for the development of science that expands beyond the known. Calmness is essential for the connection with eternity that is the birthright of the soul. The soul knows Calmness but the body requires lessons to understand what it is.

Calmness requires open senses and open senses require Calmness. They go together of necessity. The senses cannot be opened fully if there is strain to use them. The softness of open sight allows for distance view, and for seeing to the peripheral limits. Smell, as with the other senses, can be completely ignored if it is not allowed its full, soft plenitude to be opened.

The mind cannot know calmness. Of its own it will create a false calmness that in fact precludes real calmness. It will subvert the senses because it will presuppose facts, entities, and other structures that obscure, blur, or replace that which is actually available to be heard, seen, tasted, or known by the senses.

Vibrate to a nonjudgmental awareness of the senses. Think of the qualities of the opal stone for understanding the qualities of Calmness. The opal stone's vibration is keen and sharp and exists in its own shimmering state aware of its surroundings but unaffected by those surroundings. The opal is known by some to have negative qualities, and the knowledge of those negative qualities is real. It is negative if chosen for itself and its shimmering beauty alone. It will reject and subvert if it is not allowed to vibrate for the sake of its vibration alone. Symbolically this means that awareness is present for itself alone, and not for ulterior motives. It exists for itself alone and allows for the clarity of senses as the wire allows its electricity or the water its waves.

Neither despair in the lack of awareness nor exult in its presence. Rather, be open to the experience of what it may bring.

Calmness is not Love. Love is itself an eternal truth, present everywhere and is essential to the existence of the being. Calmness allows one to be closer to Love, to embrace it without selfish design. Calmness facilitates. Calmness is essential. Without it, you cannot proceed to the further lessons that expand the spirit.

Yet, Calmness is not an end in itself.

19

Calmness Further Explained

 ow can I understand Calmness in rela-
tion to Gratitude and the Truth of Love?
I asked.

*One aspect is a refinement of perception and a
more adept use of the resources of Gratitude. In
its other aspect, it is a refinement of Thought, a
distillation of Thought, and an aggregation of
Thought in relationship to the great observer
Creator, Love.*

*On the one hand, you cannot achieve a
sufficient level of attention and awareness
unless you are able to escape, at least for
sufficient periods of time, the turbulence of the*

River of Nows. The River is always turbulent
somewhere.

There are times when the turbulence of the
River cannot be avoided. The adept use of the
River and especially the adept use of Thought
as it relates to the River is to achieve levels of
perception and perspective and to allow one's
thoughts and one's influence on the physical
being to be independent of the raging forces of
the River. Stepping out of the River and looking
at it from a distance always requires an element
of Calmness.

The refinement of Thought and thus the
refinement of spirit will always grow as one
becomes more experienced in the use and
enjoyment of Gratitude. The ability to use the
River and to be attached to Gratitude in a well-
developed and mature fashion requires
sensitivity to, and mental attention to, a very
wide array of different resources.

Understanding the resources and their
interconnections in the Realm of Gratitude
demands discernment. Discernment requires
application of Thought at high levels. Opening

*one's mind, heart, and full intuition to the
Realm of Gratitude will inevitably lead to an
advancement of spirit, whether or not one is
aware of it or seeks it. This application of
Thought and observation will lead one to
greater refinement of Thought, elevating the
adept use of the Realm of Gratitude to high
levels of advanced awareness.*

*These higher levels will be accepted by Love, the
great observer, as the more powerful, if not the
most powerful, Thought. The higher levels of
Thought return power to Love, the Creator.
These levels attract a wide array of spirits and
messengers that Love has available to connect
itself to Thought.*

Aatnan went on to give me instruction on the relationship of Life, and of spirit, to Wisdom and Love.

*Spirit was born with Life, in the physical
world, in the Realm of Wisdom. The first spark
of Life involved the first thought. Love, being
everywhere in the physical world, and as the
physical world depends upon Love to exist,
Love immediately knew, when it felt the first
thought, that its kindred spirit was born. Love*

in its great and infinite power gave rise to Wisdom. Wisdom has an infinity of organization, in dimensions far beyond those you can imagine.

As Life has developed, and as Thought has grown in complexity, Thought approaches, if not achieves, an infinity of its own in its complexity.

In the instant moment of Now as it starts to enter the River or slightly after, Advanced Thought is able to connect to the Creator. This connection, with both energy and Thought, requires intention, attention, and focus. Only Calmness allows one to enter this place of connection with the Creator, Love.

Understanding where Gratitude originates, and remotely how it is interconnected with the infinite universes, requires Calmness. And, connecting with Love's power requires Calmness.

If one is in the raging River of Nows, connecting is impossible. Even approaching that point is unfeasible if the influences of the River are not placed at a distance.

20

Calmness Involves a Shift in Attention

ow does one get into the state of Calmness?

Calmness involves a shift in attention. It quiets the River and gives an opportunity to relate to the River in a way that is not only fresh but allows for a view without the turbulence and the undertow that the River always exerts when one is in the River. It is all within the Realm of Gratitude, because it involves relating to the material world. Yet, it involves a shift in Thought, a shift to a new level of observation. The level of observation allows more clarity and less passion. Thought, at this level, is more refined.

All living beings are interrelated. The Thought of all living beings is also interconnected, much like an energy field. Advancement in observation allows for enlargement and advancement of the field. The Rivers of the Now of each human involve highly advanced Thought. All the Rivers of all human beings are interrelated, some nearly running in the same channels. When the Rivers are connected, the result is often the sharing of turbulence, or at best enhancing some aspect where the Rivers intersect.

To achieve spiritual advancement, a more complete connection between humans and all of Life is a requirement. Any advancement requires humans to connect by advanced observation, coupled with advanced Thought, to Love, the Creator. Thought cannot allow for the most advanced connection when the River is sweeping you along.

Likewise, Thought does not allow for refined observation if the attention is riveted by the excesses and complexities of emotion and feeling. Only distant observation allows that. The shift to a place that has less emotion and more clarity is essential to this view. Calmness is necessary in this step in observation.

When Calmness is present, be aware of the great wealth of Gratitude. In turn, you will discover a shifting to a higher level of Thought; and observation is brought about. To go to the advanced lessons and the advanced levels of Compassion, Inclusion, and beyond, it's critical to achieve competence in Calmness.

21

Understanding and Practicing Calmness

 asked Aatnan to instruct me in the practice of Calmness.

In each and every thing that living creatures do, in every action taken, and in every instant of the movement of their very cells is the action of constant Thought. Much of the Thought is passed and gone away long before human consciousness can detect its existence.

Consciousness and feeling are the only ways of understanding, or getting a grasp on, the thinking done by human beings. Wisdom has allowed, if not fostered, this thinking that all living beings do. Wisdom in all its complexity was created by Love out of nothing. The power of Love to observe and to hold all within its grasp is much, much more than "thinking" can ever know. The powers of observation of Love, and the grasping of all within its force, are far beyond your "thinking."

You cannot think your way into an understanding of Love. You cannot think your way into an understanding of how the power of Love created the universes when nothing else existed other than itself. Yet, the paradox is that living beings created only from the physical matter of the universe, can, by the use of Thought, combine the various physical attributes of Wisdom, acquire understanding by observing, and eventually be enfolded back into the original Creator, Love.

What is important to know is that Love has embraced Thought as its own. It brings Thought back into itself and feeds on it. The powers of observation are the powers of Love. In its way, thought does observe, although crudely, and not with the force the Creator uses.

Assume that all you do in the Realm of Wisdom is thinking, because that is all that you are allowed within the constraints and boundaries of Wisdom in the Realm of Gratitude. This is all you get, yet you must, to reach spiritual Enlightenment, work within these constraints, to reach near the levels of the powers of observation that the Creator Love has. This will not come entirely by what you think is thinking.

Do not make the mistake of thinking that Love is not involved in the thoughts that living creatures have. It is involved by interaction with the thoughts of living creatures, as Love is always interested in Thought itself.

The essence of the spiritual quest is to understand why Life exists and how living creatures relate to the great universes and the force that created them. Logical human thinking about either the force of Love or the complexity of its creation, Wisdom, will always be inadequate. It will always fail to fully grasp how Life relates to the Creator and its creation. Understanding Love is possible only by the eventual enfolding back into the force of Love, and this must be done by thinking without trying to do so.

What thinking humans do is inevitably a part of the turbulence of the River of Nows. Grasping for meaning by thinking alone inevitably takes you into the River of Nows far distant from the source of Now. Do not think that it will come by thinking, and do not think that it will happen by allowing your consciousness to be swept along by the forces of the River of Nows. Understanding happens when you allow for Calmness. Calmness of thinking, in all the other ways of thinking, is the only hope you have of absorbing the meaning of your connection with Love, and its companion, Wisdom.

In times of Calmness, the thinking that you do is less affected by thinking, as you know it, and more affected by the thinking that all living beings do in their mere existence.

There is a seeming paradox in that, for you to be reconnected both to Love and Wisdom in a way that provides true understanding, Love would have you be as complex as you can be. Love would not have you change yourself at all to start the process of reconnection to Love.

 It is actually necessary that you let your River be as turbulent as it needs to be.

You are expected to be calm, stepping away from the River, all the while knowing and feeling that your River is turbulent and tumbling. The River will always be turbulent and tumbling. That is the nature of both the individual life and the nature of the interrelation of lives.

There are some things that you do in your everyday lives that are clear examples of how to work with these paradoxes. Cooking is one way of understanding it. In cooking, the mind is used, and your hands are used, in all the things that you do consciously to cook. There may be very active and even somewhat wild moments in the cooking. That wildness and extreme activity should be set aside for the eating of the food. Eating is the enjoyment and eating is the understanding of cooking. The recipe can never convey the meaning of cooking. The actual act of cooking also cannot convey the meaning of cooking.

Likewise, the great artists of history did their work and the great artists have used the various mediums over the centuries in ways that are incredibly complex and certainly must have taken a lot of "thinking" to achieve, yet the end result is not the thinking that they put into it. Rather it is the meaning that you take by seeing what was created. It is the feeling that the work of art gives you. It is a transformation in seeing, thinking, or knowing that the art will bring to you. This meaning is whatever comes to the observer without "thinking," as you would use that word. That is truly the meaning and the purpose of art.

Think, think, think and then take times of Calmness not to think. Allow your mind and senses and all parts of you to take whatever places of perception and whatever vantage point of observation they may, in order to find the true meaning of all the *thinking*. This is the reason for Calmness. It is not Calmness of a dead mind. It is Calmness of whatever actions Thought may have evoked. It is the enjoyment of what thinking has allowed. It is the paradox of being in the River, yet not being in the River.

In the River you are lost in turbulence, and may feel like you are drowning, but without the River there would be no *under-standing*. Without the River where would be those *thoughts* that may allow you to someday be reconnected to Love? How to get to that place of vantage, of being both within the River and not within the River, is the challenge of the Lesson of Calmness.

Practice Calmness by putting yourself in a place that is separate from your thinking. Put yourself in a place that is separate from your feeling that carries with it an impulse to do something. Let yourself feel what your thoughts have brought you, but only if that feeling does not bring back more thinking. Enjoy what you have made, and savor the feelings of accomplishment.

If you are seeking Calmness related to feelings of a person or a group of people, let yourself think about the person or persons but know that you are a separate person. Feel the distance of space between you and that person. Feel yourself in that empty space of separation. Be there. Then you may indulge in thinking about the relationship as seen from that space. You will inevitably feel what Calmness is about. The more you practice distance and perspective, the easier and more full it will be. Realize that the place of perspective always involves separation.

The act of awareness involves Calmness. Any enhancement of the ability to observe will involve the act of Calmness. In general, a greater distance of projection will give a clearer perspective of what is involved in the turbulence of the River, and this enhances Calmness. Also, the ability to observe from a distance requires an act of Calmness. Calmness is necessary to learn if one is to get to the more advanced observation and use of resources that understanding the Truths of Love and Wisdom requires. It is also the only way to separate sufficiently from the turbulence of the River to get to Compassion and Inclusion.

There is an irony here. The Realm of Gratitude is best enjoyed and most effectively accessed when there is separation from it and a perspective that allows it to be seen, and even felt, from a distance.

22
The Definition
of Love

Before All
And After All,
Enduring always,
Deeply knowing,
Sensing fully its creation,
Love observes,
Love supports,
Love patiently awaits
Return to it of all its own.

Atnan told me that Love and Wisdom are the two spiritual Truths. I don't know whether I was told that I would wait to learn more about the spiritual truths of Love and Wisdom or whether I just assumed that

I needed to wait until I wandered through the Lesson of Gratitude, before I started thinking about the Truth of Love. It took me a couple of years before I felt that it was the right time to ask Aatnan more about the spiritual Truth of Love. Certainly, I do love, and I have felt love. And, I assumed, as I believe most of us assume, that love is something that we know instinctively.

Love, Aatnan came to show me, is the force that created the universes. It is the force that keeps the universes intact and expanding. It is that force without which there would be no physical universes.

When I first approached Aatnan about the lesson of Love, I was thinking of the issue in human-centered terms. I asked him about the Truth of Love.

You have it and you can understand it from your own birth.

I thought this meant we all got it from the act of our creation and that we understood it in context. I imagined that the act of our own creation is connected back in the eons of time to the energy of the universe that created the first spark of Life itself. By continuing to view Love in human terms, I would be unable to understand what Love really is.

My second request of Aatnan to explain the Truth of Love was met with an obscure statement:

It is present from the act of creation, and all the connections of Life, and it is the birthright of every living creature.

I surmised that Aatnan meant that Love is present in every act of creation. I imagined that the experience of Love is felt most keenly in the intimate relationships and the close relationship that we have with other human beings and, really, in all the relationships that we have with humans and other living beings. I even began to think that Love is evidenced in all the physical matter that we see around us by virtue of and through the energy that it has, from the act of its initial creation. I thought, "It is present in the hands and minds of all humans who create anything with their hands." I continued to think of Love only as it is in relation to living beings.

This idea is not wrong, it is just very incomplete. I later came to understand that Aatnan was trying to show me how Love interacts and relates to humans and to all of Life. Yet, focusing only on the human impact of Love, I was missing the kernel of the Truth of Love.

I asked Aatnan to tell me what if anything is special about human Love.

To be human is to turn upon yourself, to be able to turn and look at yourself and to contemplate yourself.

Aatnan had not yet revealed to me that Love, as he defines the term, is essentially the ability to perfectly observe. This perfect observation is the primal force that created the universes. Without it, there would be no physical matter. Love keeps all physical matter in existence; watching, hearing and doing everything the senses do and much more. Love has the ability to know that something else exists.

Humans have powers of observation, and, in this manner, we mimic what Love does. Human observation is not perfect. It does not carry the power of Love. I came to understand that Aatnan's lesson on Love was that, if I were to look at how I am able to contemplate myself, I can get at least a minimal understanding of what Love does, constantly, in observing its creation.

Aatnan did not fully reveal the definition of the Truth of Love to me until he spoke to me later of Wisdom. He also had not yet revealed to me the important distinguishing feature of Life. When he did so, he explained to me that Life is essentially the ability to observe, and through that observation to reproduce itself. He used the term Thought to describe the ability of Life to observe and reproduce, and to describe all the actions and activities that living beings do in pursuit of their existence as living beings.

All actions that Life takes in its existence are a diminutive of Love, because all actions of Life are based on observation, in one way or another. It is all kin to Love, or put in another way, it is all kin of Love.

Love, as Aatnan uses the term, is both the all embracing and all powerful force that holds the universes together by virtue of keeping everything, even the most minute particles, in its observation. It knows that what it is holding in observation exists, even if that existence is possible only through its observation.

23
The Definition
of Wisdom

Born at the instant of Creation,
As companion to the enduring One,
Wisdom is the Rule Master,
Creating order,
And containing disorder.
Its truth supporting the Infinite
Until Love calls it back,
At the end of time.

After Aatnan began to reveal to me the meaning of the Truth of Love, I asked him if it was necessary for me to learn about Wisdom to know more about Love, and I was told the answer was yes. I asked what was Wisdom, and I was told:

Love created Wisdom when Love, acting upon itself, created energy.

Additionally, I was told that this energy began instantly to create connection, and this connection created an imperative of creation and further senses of connection. What began as the spark of Love was at once infinite and beyond mind comprehension in its immensity and its scope. Yet, immediately, by the reflection of Love upon itself, was also created a definition to the energy Love had manifested, which objectified it.

Love began to expand itself and its reach by the expansion of energy it had created. The universes are therefore the creation of Love reflecting upon itself.

Wisdom is the sense that Love has given of structure, meaning, direction, and substance, to mention only the rudimentary outlines that crude observation can find in the elegant immensity of the connections that Love has created. There is only one Love creation, but its reflection has created an infinity of connections, and also an infinity of observable universes, with an infinity of views.

All of this was made possible only through Love. Love is not the energy. Energy is the reflection of Love. Love is seen thus as an infinity of observation points, or it can be seen as more immense in scope and definition than the universes themselves.

Love created Wisdom, yet Wisdom is itself a Truth and something that must be recognized and reckoned with in its own right. This is true because what Love has created is not simply a mishmash of energy acting randomly on itself.

Love seeks itself and thereby creates a sense of direction, a sense of speed, a sense of substance, and, among its infinite reflections upon itself, an objective reality that commands a structure (for lack of a better word) that Love draws from its own design. It observed itself and found—and continued to observe and find—its own creation.

Wisdom is found in the structure of the creation of Love. As Love cannot be ignored in its own creation, neither can the many imperatives of the structure created be ignored. The Truth of Wisdom is thus seen as both the reflection of the creation of Love and the meaning in the structure itself.

24

More of What Love and Wisdom Are

 had so many questions for Aatnan. Is Love energy?

Love is that which observes. Love fills every space in the universes and it expands with every observation that it makes. Even every part of the atom has within it Love that observes what Love has created and is thereby expanded. Love actually created the physical matter of the universes. The Realm of Wisdom, what we know of as the physical universes, is kept in motion and is ever expanding.

Is Love also expanding?

Of course, but it is still no more than it ever was, and that is, the act of observation.

Does Wisdom also provide a structure to Love itself?

Yes, it does, and it is shown easily among the living creatures of the Earth, but only by the relationship, interaction, and communication of the living creatures of the Earth. Yet Love was before all, and will always be, no matter what there is to observe, or even if there is nothing to observe.

Was there something before Love and did something create Love in the first place?

There is no Truth beyond Love, and there is nothing to observe beyond that which is first observed. We cannot go deeper than that because it is the most basic principle, and the most primal act of all.

Is Love what we know of as God?

Well, Love is God and God is Love, if those are the words you wish to use to express what was

*at the beginning and what is the force that
brings together, keeps together, and is the
driving impetus of that which we know of as
the physical world. Further, Love created
Wisdom, and nothing is done in the universes,
created in the universes, or is able to be done in
the universes without the laws, the structure,
and the imperative in general of that which
is under the sway of the truth of Wisdom. If
God is Love, then God is Wisdom, and Wisdom
is God.*

Did Love create the structure of Wisdom, in the
sense that it planned the structure of Wisdom?

*As I have told you before, Love, when merely
glancing upon itself, created the force and the
energy that thereby created the universes.
The structure of that is Wisdom. So, yes, in
that sense, it was planned. The principle of
observation is infinite. There cannot be too
much to observe, and there cannot be a limit
to it.*

*It expects that which it observes will be infinite,
and of infinite structure, and capable of
expression insofar as the observation continues.*

Thus, there is no limit to complexity. There is also no limit to the Realm of Wisdom and there is no limit to the great and deep knowledge and the great and deep knowing that is Wisdom.

Is Wisdom growing in the sense of adding new parts and new aspects to its knowing?

Yes, it would have to, for the simple reason that infinite observation is always observing more. Each new theory or principle that the human mind can devise or conceive of, may, and often does, explain, but it can never explain away, because there is always a new way to observe and a new way to understand the infinite nature of the act of observation.

I realized from what Aatnan has been saying that Wisdom acting in concert with Love, which it always does, serves to provide the structure of the observation, which is the ever-expanding Love. Therefore, Wisdom is always learning more about itself. This would serve to explain why Life is in existence. It serves to explain why Life is ever expanding in its complexity.

I asked whether Love is trying to know itself, and was told:

Love is not trying to know anything. It is only trying to observe. Love lets Wisdom deal with the act of knowing. Love lets Wisdom deal with the act of planning. Love lets Wisdom deal with every act of what was, what is, and what is meant to be (or will be). Because Love is infinite in nature, and Wisdom is likewise infinite in nature, there is no limit to that which Wisdom can create, and there is no limit to what Wisdom has already created.

Are human beings the most advanced or the most developed, of self-replicating, antientropic entities in the universes?

No, certainly not. That would place limits upon what is infinite in itself, and thus it cannot be true that humans are the most developed in that regard.

25
How and Why Does Love Care?

came to see that all of Life, from the time of conception to one's death, is an adventure in the exploration of Gratitude.

Our ability to grasp even the merest fraction of the resources that are present in the instant of Now is limited by our primitive senses.

Our abilities to navigate the flow of the River of Nows are likewise limited by both the frailties of senses and the failure of adequate perspective and perception. The River is Wisdom's creation always supported by the intense attention of Love.

Our daily lives, our realities, all of our relationships and all of our emotions, together with every other aspect that we feel and think, is a creation of Wisdom, and we are bound by the River of Nows, the creation of Wisdom, at least until we exit this Earth and this earthly body.

The infinite nature of the universes and the great infinity and complexity of Wisdom are at odds with our sense of being fixed in a certain state, at any given moment of Now in the River of Nows. It is always moving; it is always changing.

I asked Aatnan if it makes sense that the instant point of Now can also be that point that connects with all of the infinite resources of the universes. I also asked if the infinite resources of the universes are available at the moment of Now to change whatever is in that moment. I wanted to know if this change in the moment could be a change to another of the infinite number of universes with which it is connecting. I asked Aatnan if that view is correct.

The moment of Now is every bit as much the act of creation as was the act of creation when the universes first began by Love observing itself. Love is now diffused in the infinitely vast creation of the universes. It continues to produce the universes in conjunction with Wisdom. The infinite resources of any universe are available, at any moment of Now, to change

that universe to another. The infinite nature of
the Realm of Wisdom requires this.

I now understand that we as living beings observe and, in that respect, partake of the elementary aspects of Love. The answers that come from Aatnan indicate that all the beings of life are connected in Love. But, one of the questions that had continued to intrigue me since I began learning from Aatnan was whether Love was specifically directing the development of Life, or whether Life has simply been created as something of the product of Wisdom. In other words, are we the workings of Love or are we merely a byproduct of what Love originally created? I asked Aatnan for advice and guidance on this point.

> *You are bound in this form. You are also bound*
> *to this form of Life in which you were created.*
> *That means that an imperative was created*
> *long, long ago that directs the life form in each*
> *of the individual entities in the many forms of*
> *Life. That imperative comes from the Realm of*
> *Wisdom. That imperative is to eat, to*
> *reproduce, and to observe. If the individual life*
> *form does not take nourishment then it will*

cease to exist as an entity. If it does not defend itself and protect what has been given to it, then it may also cease to exist by having been eliminated.

This, Wisdom knows. We cannot know the extent of Love's domain. We will never know the infinite complexity of the creation of Wisdom.

Aatnan declined to say whether Love had planned it or whether it was just a random event.

Such a quest to learn the extent of Love's domain and the infinity of Wisdom's creation is not what the spiritual quest is about.

I still had questions. Does Love care about the individual actions that we take? Or, does Love observe each individual action in a way that would connect back to itself by either judgment or some other tangible form of the act of observation? And finally, Does Love focus on us now, or did it only focus in the original act of Creation of the universes?

The power of Love's observation is much more intense than can ever be imagined. It is the power of the observation of Love that keeps the universes together and keeps it all expanding and growing. Love is obviously observing that which was created by Wisdom. Love is within each of the infinite points of the universes that have been the product of Wisdom.

Yes, Love is concerned and does, in essence, care for who you are and what you are. It is not concerned about your choice for breakfast. Likewise, Love is not concerned whether you are practicing in one religion or another, or, necessarily, whether you are practicing in any religion at all.

Love is intensely aware that it has created the observing, antientropic, concentrated energy of the Life that inhabits your Earth. Love cares intensely about your act of observation, because that, in fact, is Love instituted within you.

You are Love working itself through the physical Realm of Wisdom. Love is based in an eternity of that which was and will always be. Love will have its creation with or without you. It will have its creation from simplicity to complexity in the development of this self-observing Life form. It was set in motion and is inexorable no matter what you do.

You should be concerned with what you do with your intense powers of observation, and not with whether Love is presently observing each and every one of your acts of observation.

Be aware that you are, in fact, exercising the power of Love whenever you observe. There is a responsibility to be aware of what you are doing.

Through the Lesson of Gratitude, I realized, we learn how Love works in relationships. We can see Love working when we create with our minds or our hands. We can feel it in our hearts as we relate the power of the River of Nows to our life's concerns. We feel the connection that only comes through the powers of intense observation and awareness. All of it fits into the rushing River of Nows. All of our human activities take on a different significance when we realize that our capabilities, and the capabilities of Life itself, partake of powers of observation and awareness that are essentially divine in nature. All of the actions of Life take on a new meaning.

Aatnan admonished me to not forget how intense the power of Thought is. Thought partakes of both the structure of Wisdom and the power of the observation of Love. It is a combination of both. It is not merely the workings or the interplay between the power of Love and fixed creation of Wisdom as is found in the inanimate world. It is, instead, the marriage of the two.

 Thought reverberates and Thought endures.

Aatnan said that even though it may not seem to make sense, Love did not concern itself with what Wisdom, in fact, created by the intense energy of the act of Love observing itself. Love set about to continue the observation of what had been created. In other words, it has not taken its glance or its sense away from what was created. It just does not care intensely about whether one part of its creation is in a certain part of the universes or another. Rather, it is concerned with perpetuating it with the same intensity that first created the Realm of Wisdom.

Love is involved in all of your thoughts,
because your thoughts, and Thought itself,
would not exist without it. In the grand
scheme of things, Love does, in essence, direct
the extent, the intensity, and the direction
of Thought, but it does not concern itself, for
instance, about whether your thought today
is to praise your neighbor or to criticize
your neighbor. It only seeks to intensify the
power of observation, because that is what
Love is.

Love would have us possess more Gratitude and, in that possession, also be grateful. Love would always have us observe more effectively so that we can all interact more effectively with the resources that are given to us.

 The basis of our existence is the observation of our resources. It is fundamental to our existence.

Spiritual growth involves more than just burning through each and every resource that we find. The earliest life forms have been very good at doing just that, but to their detriment, inevitably consuming their own environment. Learning moderation in the exuberance of Gratitude is part of spiritual growth.

Aatnan told me that Love is intensely interested in the development of Thought as a combination of itself and Wisdom. Love is, therefore, concerned with the individual spiritual development of living beings. It is concern with the spiritual growth of each human.

> Love will be there urging it on.
> Love will be there for each and every act
>   of observation.
> Love will continue to provide the power and
>   the direction.

Until we reach Enlightenment we will fail in our act of observation to take in all the resources that are available in the given moment of Now. The spirit also admonished me to remember that there is no finality, there is only process.

> Love is the originator and progenitor of
>   the process.
> Love is that force which keeps the process
>   in motion.

Life, and each one of us individually, is part of that process. Until we reach Enlightenment, we cannot participate fully in all that Love does. We end up straddling the Realms of Love and Wisdom.

Is Love Diffused or Coalesced?

fter Love created Wisdom and the physical universes were created, Love became diffuse throughout the expanding universes. Asking Aatnan whether Love has stayed diffuse or whether it has coalesced into form in places in the universes, he told me to imagine it as both diffuse and coalesced.

Love is present both within and around the physical universes. In this aspect it is diffuse. As the physical universes—or as Wisdom has formed the physical matter of the universes— there is form that is built around, with, and through Love. The life forms of Earth are all

*coalesced forms of Love, organized through the
principles of Wisdom.*

*You cannot know the extent or the complexity
of Wisdom. While you are in human form you
cannot know the reasons for the existence of
spirits. Also, you cannot fully grasp the
complexity of the reasons or principles behind
that which nurtures and that which tends to
destroy, or appears to destroy.*

*Likewise, you cannot know the full process or
the intense complexity of the infinite universes
that are present in any given moment of Now.
Yet, you, in combination with other forms
of Life, do create Thought fields and energy
fields. You can commune and connect with
other living creatures and with entities of the
spirit world.*

Aatnan taught me that all spirits, all thoughts,
and all connections between living creatures have
their origins in Love. We do not realize how profound and intense the capability of perceiving and
observing fellow travelers of this Earth is. It is the
profound, deep, and intense principle of Love that
allows the observation to occur. Imperfect as it may

be, Life is Love in action as organized through the principles of Wisdom.

> *You cannot substitute your immediate judgments of what is "wise" for what are the principles of Wisdom in action. In the infinite universes, all scenarios are played and replayed with nurture, and destruction played out in them all. Your thoughts are forms of Love in the play of Wisdom. In like ways, so are spirits. All are observations organized through Wisdom. The individual thoughts that make up Thought are observations that wait to be further observed. The spirit, organized through Love and Wisdom, waits to be observed. The spirit and Thought do not exist until observed. Their form is that which is observed.*

27

Love's Connection to Thought

he lessons have taught me that Love only indirectly created thought as we know it. Love observed and created the physical universes governed by the principles and the processes of Wisdom. Love became attached to this because the force of Love could not and would not disengage from the processes that became the domain of Wisdom.

Love also did not directly contemplate and thereby create the processes that Wisdom uses. Love, for instance, did not become concerned that one atom was for the element of gold and other for lead. Love did not create experiments to decide which physical elements could attach to each other, send signals to each other, recreate their attachments, and thereby reproduce.

What Love did do was originally attach, and still stays attached, to all places in the universes. It has not taken its gaze away, nor has it diminished any of its ways of fully observing all that transpires in the physical domain. Love attached immediately to Thought, when it first appeared, and has stayed attached to it. It takes Thought to itself, reabsorbing it to its force of observation. Thought immediately connected itself to Love and began to partake, at a diminutive level, of the powers of creation that is Love's achievement.

Learning this gave rise to several questions that I brought to Aatnan.

Does Thought, by virtue of its connection to Love, and its powers of observation, partake of some mystical abilities, not explained by its own thought processes?

Do living beings in their thought processes have a right to claim dominion over the physical domain or any biosphere in the universes?

Did Love invest its own powers in
Thought and thereby facilitate increased
Thought with enhanced relationships to
the physical universes?

Did Love specifically decide to intervene
into the evolution of Life and thereby
create the unique living being that was our
first human ancestor?

I was not receiving answers to these. Finally
Aatnan told me to stop asking questions and to
listen. When I listened, *I* was asked a question. I was
asked what I thought observation was basically all
about. To answer, at first I felt as if I was looking
for something in a cluttered, unlit room. Then I
realized that the answer must be that observation is
seeking to know something.

 Knowing requires becoming conscious.

Aatnan let me know that I was answering my
own questions. I asked what knowing was, and I

was told that knowing is becoming as fully aware as possible; being as open as can be to feel what other thinkers are feeling. That means being aware of what living beings of less thought capacity are enduring; what they may be feeling; and what their experience must be. Knowing is listening, hearing, seeing, and being as much in connection as can be. That means inclusion, and extending one's self.

I returned briefly to my question of what Love's involvement is with Life as it is developing. I asked the question again whether Love was involved in the first experiment with something purely physical becoming aware of itself and reproducing. I was told that Love had been there from the inception of the universes, and, yes, there is just one universe with an infinity of forms.

Love had been seeking consciousness. Aatnan told me that Love fills itself with Love force when it finds Thought; that when Thought reaches to a certain level of consciousness there is a shift that fills Love even more. At that point the sufficiently conscious Thought returns to Love and leaves the physical plane entirely. It becomes part of Love. It becomes pure Love. It is the place of Enlightenment.

Then I was given a glimpse of what Love is.

Love is the ability to feel; to hold; to see; to listen; and to totally absorb what it is observing. It is an embrace beyond the connection of the most passionate lover. It is more than the feeling of the parent for the child. It is total absorbing without the loss of identity. It observes without judgment. It cannot seek to take anything that is not freely given. It fosters. It nourishes.

Aatnan then told me that Love did not decide the mode of the first physical connections that allowed the first spark of Life on the planet Earth. Love was, however, immediately ready to connect to it. Once Life started, Love was feeding it and encouraging it by absorbing its thoughts.

I was then asked if I wanted to learn something more. I almost thought what I had just learned was enough to try to keep together and write down, as I was sure I left some things out that Aatnan was trying to teach me. I did listen. I was given an image. It was the image of Love watching, feeling, and hearing the thoughts of the living being(s).

Then I saw another image of Love feeding the desire for more connection; the desire for more Thought; and I realized that this deep interest, deep connection, this intense encouragement is with Love always. It was present even before this universe was formed.

 Love has the desire for Thought. It has the desire to watch it grow. It also seeks to fulfill all desires of the living being. It seeks the completion of the living being. Love's desire is to actually fulfill, and fill itself. Its wish is literally for more Love.

Love will never insist on one form or another. It will never insist on one act or another. Thoughts that do not tend toward greater inclusion are not fed the desire for more growth. Those thoughts are ones that would diminish rather than increase awareness. Love does seek to direct Thought toward greater consciousness.

28
Revel in the
Love Connections
that You Are

Know that you are the highest concentration of Love connections that exist in this sphere, and know that the feelings of disconnection and confusion are only a trick of your mind when stressed and tired. The spirit would have you quiet your mind to sense the connections, animate and inanimate, that Love has made here and into the far reaches of all the universes.

Wisdom knows the rhythm of the many codes that Love spawned in the first moment of energy creation. Wisdom is the sense and Wisdom is the understanding of the structure of Love that is made from infinite connections that Love has made in its own reflection.

In every part of the smallest fragment of the universes is energy that Love sustains with its glance. There is no place in the infinite universes where Love is not found. Love is in each place and Love is all.

 You are Love and you are Love evolving.

Within Love, and in all the connections that make up Love, is found the Wisdom that followed Love's first vision of itself. This Wisdom both fills you and surrounds you. It is yours for the seeing, the hearing, the tasting, the embracing, and the all encompassing. It is not the confusion that a tired mind is feeling.

It is actually the confusion of Wisdom that is sensed when the mind is not quiet, calm and attentive. Wisdom will whisper both the equations of the most brilliant and the poems of the sensitive. It is found in the buzzing of the bees and the shaking of the earthquake.

29
Life's Connection and Obligation to Love

At first I was perplexed when trying to consider how individual Life entities were connected to Love. I had no evidence that Life's beginnings were anything other than random events. Even assuming it is correct that Love was involved with Life at its inception, due to the attraction of Love to the Thought that the Life forms were producing, what difference would this make to any individual entity? The individual entities all seem, in one way or another, to have been in a struggle to survive and to reproduce.

Although Love may be both aware of and highly interested in the activities of the Life forms, why should that make any difference to the individual Life entity? The answers did not come to me after thinking about these questions, so I took these questions to Aatnan.

He told me to remember that each Life entity is related to each other in many complicated ways. He said to remember that each Life entity is constantly involved in the act of creation by observing itself in so many complicated ways.

The constant stream of Thought, produced by each Life entity, connects intimately to Love, Aatnan said, whether or not the individual Life entity is aware of the connection. Love's embrace of Thought produced by the Life entity serves as an encouragement to that individual entity, whether or not it is aware of it. Each additional level of complexity of Life forms produces greater complexity of interaction of the entity with both itself and with those Life entities around it. This increases the awareness of Love to the entity and thereby also increases the encouragement for the collective of those entities to increase its own complexity.

As each level of complexity is reached, the ability of the Life entities to be self-reflective increases. It is through the encouragement of Love that the ability to be self-reflective increases.

Self-reflection involves the ability to change its perspective and to change its place of perception. This increases the level of Thought and thereby increases the connection to Love, the Creator. In this process, there is a great obligation of each entity to Love, the Creator. The self-reflective entity is obliged to recognize that what it is doing is a part of the universal creative process.

 The self-reflective entity is responsible for the existence of the physical universe and the presence of Life within it.

All that concerns the one who observes is present in the here and Now. The absolute instant of Now is the moment of observation. The connection of the Nows is the concern of Wisdom and is within its domain. Wisdom is perpetuated by the force of Love which is generated in the Now. Wisdom perpetuates the creation produced by Love.

 Wisdom creates continuity. Love feeds it. Love makes it move, gives it form and supports it in every way, but only from instant to instant. It fills every place, every corner of the physical world of Wisdom.

Every moment of the past and every moment to come in the future is inherent in the infinity of the moments of Now, diverging in the unlimited ways that Wisdom allows. Love embraces all in its observation, without judgment. Wisdom allows all, without judgment. Love cannot let go. Wisdom cannot discontinue or stop, as long as the force of Love envelops it.

Thought invites and allows judgment. It is the way of the living entity. We find justification for judgment in the reality of our world with such statements as:

Poison is not as good as food;

Pain is not as good as non-pain;

The stranger is not as invited as would be a member of the tribe; and

The known is better accepted than the unknown.

Love and Wisdom allow judgment, as the domain of Thought is reserved for the living entities. Yet, Love feeds all—judgmental and nonjudgmental. Love is complete, all embracing, and enveloping, whether known or not by the living entity. Thought, as a form of self-reflection, began with the first living entities, constrained to reflect as they were on how to perpetuate their kind.

Thought is always searching when prodded by necessity for better methods of entity perpetuation. At these times, self-reflection of Thought is focused in a changed perspective. Those moments are of special concern to Love, always attracted to absorb the force that is emitted by Thought. Love's appetite is only to energize creation, to hold all in its embrace. The image is one of Love replenishing itself.

Creative human thought immediately attracts Love's attention as an event of self-reflection. Creative thought is the warp speed of self-reflection and change. When creative thought embraces other living entities, it reaches to the highest levels of Love's attention, as it feeds Love at a level far advanced over limited self-reflection. Thought of all-embracing self-reflection is absorbed directly in the force of Love, losing all connection to the physical world.

All living entities are specially embraced by Love. Love does not judge the content of self-reflection. Inherent in the process of Love's special connection to Thought is the encouragement of ever more embracing self-reflection.

Creative Thought is a high form of self-reflection, favored by increased attention of the observation of Love. Sentient creatures have an obligation, inherent in their own constitution, to produce the Thought that best gives back to Love, the Creator.

30

Observation Is the Essence of Creation

Make no mistake, human creatures, that your act of observation is not something created by you for your own self-interest or self-aggrandizement. It only seems that way because you taste, you feel, you see, you hear, you touch, you think, you apprehend, and you are aware. It only seems that it begins and ends with you.

On the contrary, you, and all humans, and all living creatures interacting in the physical, are intimately connected to the manifestation of Love's continuing observation. Love does not observe only as would a clinician, or a jeweler, making a diagnosis or an appraisal to be *reported to another. Love's observation is the essence of the act of creation, as its observation embraces, upholds, and strengthens all that its great powers of grasping can allow. It holds together each atom, and each smaller part that holds the atom together. It gives form and substance to all matter. Love creates the whirl of energy, as Wisdom creates the physical atoms you see.*

Your act of observation, although focused, and not omnipresent as is Love's, has with it, nonetheless, the great power of holding together that which it observes. Therefore, what you apprehend, and what you hold close to you, is always affected by you.

Embrace what you observe. Each speck of what you observe has more of the power of observation than you will ever have, as it is Love undistilled that is holding that speck of matter together. Know that each living creature that you encounter is an active entity manifesting Love in the physical world and holding matter also in its power of observation. Best it is not to arrogate too much importance to a power to destroy what one observes.

Bear in mind that ignoring what you are observing is defaulting on the obligation that the power of observation requires, and that is, namely, to embrace and to realize that your observation is part of the primal act of creation itself.

31

Thought's Connection to Love

The relationship of Thought to Love and Wisdom was something that concerned me for weeks. I could not figure out how to think of Thought in relation to the physical world, since it is so different from it. I could not figure out how Thought related to Love. Was Thought an outgrowth of Love, fostered and cultivated by it? Or, was it something that Love came to recognize and relate to after its presence became known? After I had thought about it for a time I took the questions to Aatnan.

Your physical bodies come straight from the Realm of Wisdom. It is always in service to it, and you are always under its influence, if not always its control. The Realm of Wisdom is one of great complications. Its intricacies and its interrelationships are infinite in complexity. The origin of Thought was literally about how to perpetuate the living being within the Realm of Wisdom. Thought always extended beyond itself and surrounded all living beings, once Thought was first created with the beginnings of Life. Primitive Thought did little more than cover the primitive beings in a loose net of Thought.

As Life became more self-reflective, it gained in its ability to become more effectively connected with other living beings. It literally created and continues to create an aggregation of varied living beings with different functions operating in one whole. The different parts of the complex living being serve very different purposes. The beating heart and the toenail do not have much in common as far as function is concerned. Yet they both serve the whole. The Thought that connects the various parts and various energies of the complex living being is far from a loosely connected net.

Thought within the complex living being is complicated beyond imagination. Much of what you think of as "thought," that is to say, the various impulses and notions you have from minute to minute are the deceivingly simple conscious parts of your thought. The thoughts that your body creates, which is part of the greater Thought, are extended far beyond you. They connect to all the living beings and they connect, of course, with Love immediately as a kindred and nourishing spirit for Love itself.

Thought is always in service to Life, whether or not it seems that way to your limited conscious mind. It is due to the extreme complication of Thought that the conscious mind of the human being is so limited and scattered. The Thought that humans engage in at the deepest limits and the most complicated levels are far beyond what the conscious mind can grasp. Thought at the deepest levels is connecting to the whole of not only the living being itself, but with all of Life.

At the conscious level of your thoughts there is the necessity of connecting with all the varied parts and the varied functions of the being. There is insufficient capacity to connect with the whole of being, and certainly insufficient capacity to connect with the Thought field that connects all living beings.

Love is always encouraging you to extend your own observation by means of Thought. Love encourages Thought to allow you to gain in your complexity. This allows you to have higher levels of Thought to increase the depth and the extent of your observation. Self-reflection always requires that you extend yourself beyond yourself, to look back upon yourself to see how better you can connect yourself both to yourself and to those living beings and the Realm of Wisdom around you.

The more aware you are, the more you are able to grasp and use the resources present within the Realm of Gratitude.

The infinite amount of resources that you have available cannot be made available without Thought and cannot be made available without orderliness.

As the Lesson of Gratitude revealed, there is no access to the Realm of Wisdom except in the moment of Now, which of course is so infinitely small that grasping it is impossible. Love exists in and operates in the infinitely small moment of Now. Wisdom knows how to keep it going and Love cannot help but feed this Realm of Wisdom. One could say that Love is in service to Wisdom, as that is certainly the effect of it. One could also say that Love stays connected to the physical world by observing it. That is what Love does. It is the all-embracing force of Love that is the reason for the existence of the universes.

If you are to connect with Love it must be in the instant moment of Now. That is not a true connection because it is gone before you ever knew you could be there. The Thought that connects you with Love is more of an opening of your awareness to the infinity and the immense power of the moment of Now. This may bring clarity to the conscious thoughts that you have in the contemplation of the moment of Now. It also gives you a glimpse or a sense of how your universe, which you know in the River of Nows, is connected to all the other universes, which are infinite in number. It certainly does allow you to more effectively direct your life to use the resources that are available in the Realm of Gratitude.

It is because your thoughts are in the service of the perpetuation of the Realm of Wisdom that your thoughts do not easily, if ever, connect directly to the moment of Now. They do not, therefore, connect directly with Love in that instant moment where all of the universe is being observed and perpetuated by the force of Love. Love is holding you up physically, and the thought that you are producing as a living being comes after that. The force of Love and Thought are not directly connected.

The Lesson of Calmness helps to bring that connection of Thought and Love closer together. Your racing thoughts that are connected to the River of Nows cannot serve you in the desire to connect with Love. That desire to connect with Love began with the very first spark of Life. Life races to connect with Love.

One cannot be in a state of Calmness unless one is also in a state of high energy. No energy, in absolute calmness, would be death. Every level of Thought in every living being involves the expenditure of energy beyond what you can imagine. You are an energy-producing factory. The fact that it is so well controlled belies the power of the living being, and certainly the power of each human being. Expect the state of Calmness to be one of excitement and a sense of high energy. Limit it as close as you possibly can to the instant moment of Now. This will keep it as separate as possible from the tumult of the River of Nows. The River is certainly a place of high energy. It is the aggregation of the infinite number of Nows that came before it, and it is the anticipation of the infinite number of Nows that there will be in the future.

Being calm means to let go of the past and to not be concerned with the future. The future will all take care of itself as it unfolds. It certainly has an infinite array of possibilities of where it may ultimately lead each living entity, and where it may lead all of Life itself.

The closer you bring your Thought to the moment of Now, the more expansive that Thought can be. Your Thought will be more expansive because it will be able to more effectively connect to the infinite resources of the moment of Now. The moment of Now is infinitely short, but not infinitely small in terms of its connections to the universes. It is a

175

paradox that the closer one brings one's self to the infinitely short moment, the more expansive and comprehensive your Thought can be.

What you call thoughts in the River of Nows are frequently very short and very limited as they are connected always to the confusion and disconnected nature of the racing River of Nows. Calmness requires stepping out of the River to get a vantage point different from that afforded within the River.

All advances of Life have been achieved through complexity of Thought. The complexity has always involved new multi-levels of physical observation. This has allowed for sensing the physical world differently than was allowed before. The advanced thought process of the human being allows you to gain a different vantage point, at any given time you wish to do so.

Indeed, focusing on the instant moment of Now is not something that the River of Nows would ever lead you to do. Only by, in essence, stepping away to observe something other than the racing River can you gain a sense of where the point of Now is, and what it has and what it affords. Away from the River you can find Calmness.

The closer you get to the moment of Now, the more energy you can feel. The closer you bring your thoughts to the moment of Now, the larger and more extensive those thoughts can be, because they connect to the moment of Now with its infinite connections to the other universes. It is a paradox that the closer you bring your thought to the infinitely short moment, the bigger and more extensive your thought can be.

32

The Heart's Access to Love — How Miracles Happen

While still working with the first Lesson of Gratitude, I asked Aatnan what re-lation the heart center would have in both the exploration and the sense of Gratitude. I was told that the heart center would be an indispensable place to sense the full extent of the resources available at any time.

The heart is essential for attaching, for creating, for connecting, for accessing the many resources available in the universe that have not yet been made apparent or manifest. The heart is a necessary part of the close and intimate connection with other lives, and other life forms. It creates a path to and a way of understanding the universal truth of Love.

 The heart reveals how understanding and using the infinite resources of the Now are interwoven in a web with so many complicated and seemingly contradictory thoughts and sentiments.

The heart holds an intelligence that the mind does not have. It connects the head with the other parts of the human repertoire of energy/thought, intelligence/being and many perhaps yet unknown ways of interacting with self and the universe. It, like the brain, has untapped energy and potential.

Opening the heart means tapping into energies and feelings that will not likely be consistent or harmonious with thought programs and patterns that have become the conventional wisdom of the existing social structure. It will thereby create discomfort, if not worse, for the individual brave enough to open it for exploration and use.

The heart is always there. But, it can be displaced by ignoring it or by allowing one's self or others to act contrary to the heart's desire or intention. Life in any social structure is nearly always a constant struggle against the intentions and desires of the heart. The heart is not always benign or congenial to others. The lessons it has to teach may be a harsh rebuke, or worse, to the social network in which one finds one's self at any given time. The heart cannot be ignored or hidden away forever. It will make itself known directly or indirectly.

Yet the heart is an integral part of any experience. The Now cannot be fully connected without access to and through the heart. The heart, with its connection to the Now, will give us access to the infinite resources of the universes. The Realm of Gratitude is built with these resources. The heart connects to all feelings. It allows us to attach and is always involved with detachment. In Aatnan's words:

Attach with awareness; connect with a sense that connection will not be exclusive to any one thing, person, or thought. The heart connects with Love, the Creator, from which all resources are available.

As you access different resources from the Realm of Wisdom, resources which have been made available through the input of Love, you will, inevitably and correspondingly, shift your universe and change it to another.

The heart connects to Love, and Love provides.
The infinite array of resources available, through
Love's creation at any given moment of Now,
is beyond the knowing of either your heart or
your mind.

You form your intentions and desires with both
your mind and your heart. Only the heart can
manifest those intentions and those desires.
When those intentions and desires are
connected with Love, at the instant moment of
Now, resources are made immediately available,
to be manifested, as the processes of Wisdom,
in the River of Nows, allow. Wisdom may work
to manifest those intentions and desires
immediately, or it may take time before it does.

Aatnan also told me that if one expects intentions
and desires to connect with Love, in the moment of
Now, it must be done with intentions and desires
that are intensely felt and with a full sense that those
intentions and desires will be heard by the Creator.
I realized that Aatnan was talking about what reli-
gions have called "faith." It is an unwavering sense
that what one can see, hear, and feel, in one's heart
and mind, once given to the Creator, will come to

pass in time. The weaker this faith, the less likely the intentions or desires will be manifested.

It has been usual to limit the word "miracle" to describe only the most unexpected or highly unlikely of events. Aatnan wanted it known that all events affecting living beings, whether unlikely or expected, are all events that come to pass because Love has acted in response to intentions or desires, expressed through Thought. Aatnan told me many times that Love takes Thought to it by an innate, and instantly bonded, attraction. Thought is of Love's own kind.

 According to Aatnan, all acts that result from the interaction of Thought involve the input of Love. All births involve miracles. All events of the life cycle involve miracles. This is true for the simplest of life forms and those that are too complex for our understanding.

Aatnan stressed to me many times that thought is part of the greater field of Thought. The thoughts produced by humans are far more than just those perceived consciously. All human thought is of the most complex and far reaching. Yet it is of the same kind as that which makes up all of Thought. It is not different in kind. All Thought reaches to, and is absorbed by, Love.

Remember, all Thought involves miracles, because it is all part of the most highly improbable of all events. It all involves connection with and eventually re-absorption to Love. The lame who give away their canes and walk are no more improbable in the grand scheme of things than the simplest plant or animal form dividing into a new being.

Aatnan wanted it made very clear that human thought is always connecting to Love. It is always influencing Love to give resources in the instant moment of Now to be added to one's River of Nows. Aatnan also wanted it made clear that one must be careful with one's thoughts and feelings, because they can affect much more than is known.

Want what you truly desire, and desire what you truly want. Decide to truly live your intentions, with all your heart, and they will come to pass.

33
The Deep Well

 he focal point of the Now, in the River of Nows, is a place where the infinity of possibilities of the great past are distilled to the reality of your Now. The infinity of your future self is brought to you, just as a tractor beam pulls the object of its focused attention.

You, the aggregation of all this, much more than the magnificent brain can ever know, scan the future mostly for the known and the familiar.

> The heart brings to it that which is always a brilliant show of how varied are the combinations of resources that the universes have in abundance beyond the ends of time and distance.

In each moment of Now are combinations and choices that attract, detract, tantalize and often confuse. The choices are empowering, giving always the feeling, when tapped, that anything can be; thus, making it seem that anything wished for is a fine complement to those salient, important parts of what has been. Great stuff is that which comes from the attraction to the focus in the River of Nows.

What you would have with all your heart and with the power of your immense cerebral computer is frequently, if not often, yours for the impassioned asking. What you wish is in your grasp when the focused Now brings its past distilled possibilities to specific combinations in the future that are seen, felt, tasted, and in all ways absorbed to the complete and inner being.

What more, I asked Aatnan, should I know of this, which seems so elegant and so complete in the feeling of its inevitable being? The words I was given by Aatnan were:

The deep well.

I asked Aatnan what was meant by this. He told me that a way to understand what the focus of the Now is, as far as its consequences and its meaning for each searching soul, is that each is a great and deep well, connected to the great and deep ocean of our creation; filled with more than any of us will ever know; and with combinations, needs, forces, and varieties of resources more complete than the imagination could ever entertain.

Attention and wisdom are the words to keep in all aspects of being in the focused Now, for that which presents itself as the River of Nows is more than just the points that we know make up its vast River. It is also the waves of the River, with the confluence of other Rivers, and the influences of the universes that it brings to our senses.

Thus, the answer is that each choice of possibilities carries with it consequences that move the waves of the great River. Even the smallest choice, made without thinking but with deep assurance that all we ask for gives us the stability of the past, has consequences far beyond that which we can know. Those decisions with intense feeling and deep thought have the power to move the great River all the more.

Each emotion that comes in the hopes and the grasping of future memories has deep connection to the great well that is each of us. Each feeling is much more than we can ever imagine and, although we know some of the reactions these emotions can bring, we can never know what each reaction and each diversion that this will cause to the waves of the River.

It would seem a bit odd that great happiness and great joy should be held also with the feeling of great attention and great awareness, with Love and Wisdom, yet that is the admonition given.

PART THREE

The Lesson of Compassion

What are your feelings and emotions
That you run from
or that you use to hide behind,
But the key to the core of your inner being,
The secret lessons to find the all of you.

34
Compassion
Prerequisites

The third lesson that Aatnan had for me was on Compassion. In explaining this Lesson, he said that a full awareness of the Realm of Gratitude, and an understanding of where your River of Nows has its turbulence, is the essential foundation for undertaking the exercise of Compassion. The reason, he said, was that there is no basis for exercising Compassion without awareness of the source of emotional turmoil in your own River.

Before undertaking the Lesson of Compassion, I had thought compassion was a synonym for a sort of deep kindness with an attempt at understanding someone else. That is a common understanding of compassion, and the Lesson of Compassion certainly encompasses that. Yet, that is not the fundamental core of the Lesson of Compassion.

It is to discover where your own River of Nows has you tumbling around issues that involve the intertwining of the Rivers of one or more other living beings. Those are the turbulent places that bind you the most and are the most difficult from which to be extricated.

Those are the ones involving a parent that may have been too enmeshing, such as a mother who did not let you have your own life but wanted you to be more exclusively part of hers. It would be the one involving a father who was physically or emotionally abusive. It would be the turbulent spot involving a lover who let you down and left you there, hurt and unable to recover. It is the spot where a teacher who was cruel, or where fellow students may have harassed and bullied you. It may be the place where you were cruel, or where you let someone down and you have held a sense of deep guilt as connected to that person.

It will always be a place where some part of you never has been able to integrate with the rest of you. It may well be a place where you have hidden yourself from shame or guilt or some other strong emotion. It is probably something for which you would be embarrassed to stand in front of a crowd and give a confession.

 Compassion is a place in you that deeply longs to be opened, expressed and included.

Aatnan dedicated the Lesson of Gratitude to these parts of you that you can find yourself some-day complete within yourself.

Connecting with emotion and feeling is the essence of Compassion. Aatnan let me know that Compassion is to be done while exercising Calmness and while being as fully aware as possible of the resources of the Realm of Gratitude. Fully aware of one's existence, and viewing one's River of Nows with a variety of calm perspectives, is the ideal start-ing point for exercising Compassion. Compassion is clearly to be undertaken in earnest only with the discipline of the Lesson of Calmness and the energy and the grounding of the Lesson of Gratitude.

To undertake it without the discipline of the Lesson of Calmness is to risk being drenched in someone else's River and losing the energetic con-nection with your own moment of Now.

Compassion is as native to the instincts of the human as is the urge of the infant to suckle. We do it naturally with our family, friends, lovers and animals that we have taken in as objects of affection. We do it naturally by mixing them in with our own River, making them part of our own River.

It is easy to do with one whose River is running mostly in one's own channel. Such Compassion does not have the purity and clarity of that taught by Aatnan in the Lesson of Calmness.

The Lesson of Compassion requires connection to the moment of Now, in calm awareness of the extent of your own physical and material connections. Calmness is essential, because Compassion requires being aware of your own feelings and emotions while concurrently connecting to the feelings and emotions of another.

The exercise of Compassion requires that your own emotions and feelings be held separate from those of other. Although the River of Nows would, for you, ordinarily have mixed and intertwined those emotions and feelings, you must take care in exercising Compassion that those of the other not be absorbed with yours.

A most important reason to exercise Calmness while attempting Compassion is that you must always, first and foremost, exercise Compassion for yourself. Whatever you have done, and however you have felt, you did it in a reaction that was reasonable for you at its inception. However long you have held yourself in the place of turbulence, or a place of hiding, you have done it for reasons that a part of you has felt well justified in so doing.

 Compassion allows you no room for self-blame.

It requires you to be aware of yourself, to understand yourself and bring all feelings and emotions about any part of yourself within a place that accepts without blame. It makes you start a connection with yourself in anything that feels separate and apart.

The turbulence of the River will inevitably have someone else connected to you. Staying in connection with yourself, and allowing reasonable connection with the other, while staying effectively apart from that other, does require practice.

Aatnan suggested one way to do this is to use the throat chakra and the chakra above the heart to connect in Compassion with the other being. This does allow a tight emotional connection while also allowing you to lift, and keep, your own emotions and feelings above your own River. It gives you the opportunity to be aware of the feelings and emotions of the other as cleanly disentangled as possible.

This gives the River a chance to run more clearly and less turbulently. The effect is to allow the emotions and feelings to be cleansed and calmed, at least for a time. It allows the body, mind, and soul a time to heal.

A requirement of the Lesson of Compassion is to understand, in whatever way you can, the emotions and feelings of the other(s) with whom you are connected. It will always be your projection, but the assurance is that you will feel, or sense, something that gives you an insight into the other.

Aatnan insisted that when performed carefully and as fully as possible, this understanding of the feelings and emotions of another acquire a great significance. If it is done appropriately and with care, it can be done without risk of harm and without risk of clogging one's own River with yet more emotional turbulence. It is appropriate to do this when you are calm.

In other words, it will be when you have, by practicing Calmness, stepped away from the River long enough to allow freedom from the feeling in your head, your throat, your heart, or your gut, that something is not comfortable or is not right. If you persist in such feelings, you must rest, breathe, and meditate on your heart or practice seeing yourself from a distance away from the emotion of the River. If you cannot accomplish freedom from burdening feelings, and if you have any doubts you cannot do so on your own, you will need someone well practiced in methods of calmness, such as a meditation teacher or experienced counselor.

If you proceed carelessly, the effect may well be the opposite of what you desired. You may cause the turbulence of the River to increase, at least temporarily, and you're uncomfortable; worrisome feelings will seem strong for a time.

Take your time with this exercise. You will get better each time you practice it. Some turbulent places will more quickly yield to this practice, while others will take many sessions before you can begin to feel free from the emotion that the turmoil and turbulence has habitually brought to you.

35

Why Compassion?

asked Aatnan, Why is Compassion
necessary to deal with the intersection
of one's River with that of another? Why would it
not be enough to calmly relate in the appropriate
perspective with one's own River, and ignore the
involvement with another, and simply move on?

> *Observation is the source of creation.*
> *Observing the emotions and feelings of another*
> *with one's own feelings and with Compassion,*
> *tainting them as little as possible with your*
> *own feelings and emotions, allows you to have*
> *an observation with the greatest possible*
> *clarity. Observation can create and it also can*
> *change that which it observes. Observation*
> *renews and has a cleansing effect.*

*Thought is at the very essence of Life. Thought
allowed for the existence of Life and it
perpetuates the creativity of Life. Thought
enhances and perpetuates Love. Love thrives on
it. The force of Love draws on Thought, which
both produces and perpetuates Life.*

*Thought is not limited to mental activity in
your brain, although all of Thought is
intimately connected to the great power and
complexity of the human brain. Feelings and
emotion direct mental activity. They absorb
mental activity. They motivate mental activity.
They make much of mental activity possible.
Most importantly, feeling and emotion, and not
mental activity per se, allow one to connect to
Love, the great Creator. In so doing, they allow
for connection to the infinity that Love's force
created. They are the source of invention and
discovery through the heart's connection to
Love's infinite universes.*

*This is not mere poetry. This is not flight of
fancy. This is the reality at the edges of our own
physical world. This is truly the essence of the
Realm of Gratitude, as the Realm of Gratitude
would not contain its wealth of resources were*

it not for the creation that happens in each infinitely small moment of Now. Without access to emotions and feelings one cannot get near the instant point of Now. One should not expect feelings and emotions to be separated from mental activity, nor should one expect the contrary either. They come in a package.

Thought is not something that exists in a vacuum. It is intense, it travels through time and space without the constrictions of the physical world, and it can reach across the universes instantly. Thought connects to all of the individual thoughts of all living beings. It feeds on itself as it grows a field of Thought energy around it.

Thought tends to be bound into the River by emotions and feelings. It has difficulty escaping the River. Compassion allows emotions and feelings to be freed, at least for a time. This freedom has an effect on creativity that is immense and powerful.

Thought is raised to a new level. Observation is at an enhanced level. Love becomes more intensely interested in what is happening at these enhanced levels. It has the effect of raising consciousness and raising awareness. This level can only be called more advanced.

That is the essence of the reason for exercising Compassion.

36

The Great and Practical Benefits of Compassion

Atnan told me that each individual human has a private connection to Love. Each individual human, therefore, has a private connection through Love to all the universes. You do not connect to the universes through others. You only connect to the universes through your own private connection with Love.

Human beings are no different from other living beings in their connection to the Thought field from which all Life arises, and which connects all of Life. Much of this Thought is something that we are never consciously aware of.

It is Thought that forms the basis of the existence for Life.

The Thought field that surrounds Life on Earth is more intricately connected and complicated than mere words can ever explain. Further, humans have little understanding of the Thought field, as the connections of the Thought field are beyond their usual feelings and senses.

Aatnan told me that most, if not all, of Thought connections of the living beings on the Earth will never be consciously known and will never be seen.

According to Aatnan, each individual human is a Thought factory of the most immense complexity and each human rivals in his ability to compute and to think with even the complexity of the universe itself.

Love has created a connection for each individual human through the instant moment of Now. Aatnan showed me that this connection is through the sensory focal points of the human body, most importantly the heart chakra. At those points, there is an uninterrupted and constant contact with Love. With practice, those points can be accessed with conscious input.

Love is aware of, and monitors, all input—conscious and unconscious.

The entire body is sensitive to Love, as are all living beings. Love seeks out those connections and provides both a support and a conduit to facilitate the giving over to Love of all the observations and all the thoughts that the individual living entity produces.

Each individual cell of the human body should also be considered an individual living being in this respect. The many trillions of cells in the human body all work together in concert to support the body, to nourish the body, and to provide the body with the energy and thoughts that allow the body to work as one dynamic and powerful entity. It is at this level, through the focal energy points of Now, that Love concentrates its connections to the individual being.

By virtue of the energy/thought connection at the point of Now, each individual human is able to have input to and thereby affect its connection with Love. At this connection with Love, the individual is able to influence what Love provides from the infinite possibilities of the universes. Rest assured that Love is always providing, but it may be the same thing you have always gotten and not what you might want if you were to concentrate your desires and your intentions.

Aatnan told me that all of our thoughts have an effect on the Thought field. The thoughts that we have include all the feelings, emotions and body sensations that our minds register. They also include thoughts at a level below our conscious attention.

We cannot know the extent of our own thoughts, and we certainly cannot know the extent that our thoughts have on the Thought field. Some thoughts will have such a profound effect that the entire field is changed in a fundamental way. Most thoughts will serve to keep the field stable.

All thoughts connect to the Thought field through Love. This connection is constant and uninterrupted. Love's essential connection to Thought is to absorb it as its own. It can be considered a monitor of Thought, sensing it and providing shifts in the universe to accommodate what Thought has produced.

What we think of as miracles are the changes that have shifted the universe we were in through changes in the Thought field as mediated by Love, the Creator.

Aatnan said that miracles happen with much greater frequency than we can know. There are infinite possibilities available at any instant of Now. Love has all infinite possibilities available at any instant moment of Now. All humans influence what is available at any given moment.

Again I asked Aatnan why we need to exercise compassion if we all have such influence in what happens to any universe we are in by our thoughts and our intention. If we are so powerful in our connection through Love with the universe, why worry about being compassionate or connecting with someone else? Why not just change oneself and one's universe, and get all of the things that one wants?

Yes, indeed, you can do this, and yes, you should do what you can to influence your world and your universe through your connection with Love, because that is what Love would have you do. This is the reason that the connection has been allowed by Love. That connection, and that capability, does not take you out of the Thought field, or out of your River of Nows. It does not change the fact that while alive in this body you are firmly and deeply rooted in the Realm of Gratitude.

*That Realm partakes of the characteristics and
the rules of Wisdom. There is continuity in the
physical universes and there is a connection
that cannot be avoided while in that physical
existence. Wisdom keeps the rocks on the
mountainside from exploding. Wisdom allows
force in the dynamite to have the explosion
when it is to happen. There is continuity and
there is predictability to the physical world.*

*There is also an infinity of these continuities,
such that there is no world we could invent that
would or could ever explain how vast are the
connections that Wisdom has been given by the
force of the observation of Love. So how can you
be other than in awe of this vastness?*

*Yet in this vastness do not forget that you are
intimately and intricately connected with many
living beings, both close to you and far away.
Those connections affect you more than you can
know. If those connections are only as you
know them, and as you feel them, in your River,
you may never understand them. Even more
importantly, you may never be able to influence
them or separate from them to allow yourself
the opportunity to connect your thoughts and*

*intentions to Love. You are in the Thought
field, but it is more than likely affecting you,
and not the other way around.*

Compassion, I came to see, is an eminently practical concept. One's River of Nows is filled with a multitude of influences over others. This is a reality of the River that cannot be avoided. Compassion alone allows one to work with and influence the other Rivers that intersect, connect and influence one's own River. Compassion is the powerful tool that allows one to focus one's power of observation and understanding in a way that assists the other living being(s) with whom or with which one is connecting. It also allows, when possible, one's own being to be enhanced, reinforced and strengthened by the other living being(s) with whom one is connected.

Compassion requires sensing and feeling when observing another living being. It compels each of us to lift our self out of the entanglements of the River of Nows with an observation that focuses on where the interconnected others are at, in that moment. This focus of the observation is a power moment. In that power moment, observation is enhanced. One may think of it as a moment of higher perception.

That power moment has a new focus of observation, which will always allow a shift in both one's own River and the River of the other. This shift serves all those whose Rivers are connected at that focus of observation. This truly involves the influence and infinite possibilities of Love, the Creator. Certainly, this is a merciful act. It serves the purposes of Love to perform Compassion. It does so by enhancing the powers of observation and the powers of connection in ways that elevate the thought of the individual who is acting in Compassion and the one to whom compassion is directed.

Compassion can thus be seen as something that is truly essential for the development of each individual human. The benefits provide much more than simply the unction that the moral approval brings.

Spiritual development requires that one cultivate the capacity of Compassion and that this be exercised with frequency. It has the practical result of allowing us to work effectively in one's River and to be as full and complete as one can be. It allows one to work to higher connections with Love and thus allows, to be sure, a deeper connection with Love in the moment of Now.

In the view of this spirit, the deeper connection enhances one's spiritual place and brings one naturally to a deeper connection with the Creator. The Creator desires a deeper connection and a deeper development of the observation of Life. It serves the interests of Love to do this. In this respect, one can see the goodness, if that term can be used here, as more than just something that pleases. It is rather something that is both essential and practical.

PART FOUR

The Lesson of Inclusion

The all of you
Are discontent
When separated
From its core,
Parts are wandering far,
Or barred from the entrance.
Included all must be.
Deep Gratitude
and Divine Nature
accepts nothing less.

37
The Need for
Inclusion

 atnan told me that the fourth Lesson, the Lesson of Inclusion, focuses on bringing back into your integral self all the parts of you that may have been isolated, separated, or ignored. In the process of integrating all the parts of yourself, you will eventually and of necessity include in your life, and the core of your heart, all the other living beings that are important to your life.

This part of the Lesson from Aatnan came as a surprise to me. When he first told me that there was a Lesson of Inclusion, I assumed it meant the inclusion in my life of all those worthy persons I might meet who would need my love and attention. As with my misapprehension regarding Aatnan's meaning of Compassion, I assumed Inclusion was something that I give, not something that would primarily *involve* me. I learned that, as with Compassion, it is first and foremost about finding yourself and then how you relate to those beings whose existence has become intertwined with yours.

Does one need Inclusion? Aatnan explained that the four lessons build on each other. For those unique and fortunate souls who find all their spiritual needs fulfilled in the Realm of Gratitude, doing so calmly and without upset of any kind, learning the lessons of Calmness, Compassion, and Inclusion are unnecessary. These individuals are finding all they need in their world.

For those who find that they cannot live in the Realm of Gratitude without feeling the anxiety, pain, and upset of the turbulence of the River of Nows, Calmness is essential to extricate from that tumult. Likewise, when Calmness does not suffice to give one sufficient perspective of observation to allow the problems and issues of the River to be understood to the point that they no longer perturb, Compassion is a necessary step to deal with that set of issues or problems.

If the exercise of Compassion gives enough comfort to the heart and mind so that the problem or issue loses its issue and no longer upsets any part of the body, the Lesson of Inclusion is not a necessary step.

However, for the important issues, and the issues that continue to cause distress, Inclusion is an unavoidable step if the problem or issue is to be resolved. When that point is reached, it must inevitably involve a part of one's self that has been ignored in its intention or its desire. That is when the separated part of one's self is brought to the focus and power of the heart's connection to Love, allowing the infinite possibilities of the universe to provide a solution that fits with the intention and desire of that part.

Aatnan was very clear in the teaching that spirituality is grounded in the Realm of Gratitude.

There can be no spirituality without a clear understanding of one's world and without a clear understanding of how all of the other living beings in one's life relate to oneself. Everything that we as living beings have is a consequence of the ongoing process of the rules of Wisdom. Life's powers of observation are a result of the processes of Wisdom and they are what connect us fundamentally to our Creator.

The Thought that arose from the initial process and that has continued through to the human beings is something that has engaged Love, the Creator. This adds to the fundamental force of Love in the universes. It is a fact of our complexity as human beings that we find ourselves separated into parts that do not always seamlessly interrelate and which do not always connect as well as they could with the core of our being.

Parts of ourselves that are kept separate diminish our ability to fully relate in the Realm of Gratitude and to relate directly at the source of Gratitude with Love.

 Inclusion is the essential tool for reabsorbing the separate parts.

The practice of Inclusion allows one to be aware when the problems and issues that one is facing are a result of internal struggles of a part or parts of one's self that have been separated, isolated, or ignored.

The body and the mind give signals when something is not fitting with the core of one's being.

Those cues or signals may come from a gut feeling, a heart feeling, a feeling in the throat, a feeling in the forehead, a pressing feeling on the top of one's head, or a disquieting issue (usually of long standing) in one's mind that cannot be resolved.

Inclusion cannot happen without being well grounded in the Realm of Gratitude and without being able to effectively practice Calmness and Compassion. It is not a process unto itself. Therefore, Inclusion means bringing all the parts of one's self to one's core being, while at the same time acknowledging and even bringing into one's being those other living beings and other thoughts that are essential to the fulfillment of that part of one's self.

Aatnan taught me that the core of one's being is always where Love, the Creator, connects with the person. I was shown that this place is in the heart. Aatnan did not tell me that this is the only place where one's connection with Love, the Creator, is. It is possible that one may find another appropriate place in one's body to connect with the Creator.

The universes are supported by Love. All change happens in the universes through Love. All of Thought is being monitored by Love. As an ongoing and uninterrupted process Love fulfills every need that the living being has that allows its perpetuation. Love connects with every living being even at the most minute levels of activity of each cell.

Isolated parts of one's self do not effectively communicate with Love, the Creator. Repressed desires and repressed intentions do not connect with one's core being. Repressed desires and intentions can literally become malignancies that grow aside and apart from one's core being, and can then live only to destroy the rest of the being. By inviting the isolated parts into one's core being, one engages the power of Love to fulfill the intentions and desires and to thereby bring that fulfillment to that part and to a re-incorporation of that part into one's core being.

Love assists every living being in its living processes. Human beings are able to focus their intentions and desires, and can thereby, with the assistance of Love through connection to Thought, actuate and effectuate what are the subjects of the intentions and desires. Love does this without judgment.

Aatnan told me that, although Love desires the full reuniting of all living beings, it supports all actions, intentions, and desires of living beings. Love allows each individual to find his or her own way to Enlightenment. Love also allows human beings to fail to reach the higher levels of perception and observation.

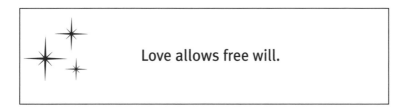

Love allows free will.

Aatnan taught me that being whole and connected in one's core being is essential to advanced spirituality. The practice of Inclusion is the method that Aatnan taught me to allow one to become whole and complete.

38

Compassion as the Prelude to Inclusion

Aatnan has said that the lives of all living beings are connected by Thought. For members of a species the thoughts are much more direct than are the thoughts between species, but there is a web that connects all of Life. The thought within a species is always fundamentally about the perpetuation of the existence of that species. There is thought communication between species through the elementary language of Life. Our thoughts are really a very limited form of Thought based only on the languages that we use to communicate verbally with each other.

Humans are reluctant to realize that emotions are both a form of thought and a type of language.

Emotions are translated and transferred by communication in many ways that we do not understand. Most of us are virtually unaware of the Thought present in other living beings and the Thought field that surrounds and radiates from all of Life.

All actions of Life produce Thought on a constant basis. Love recognizes and absorbs all of Thought, and this absorption helps to perpetuate living beings. Love communicates with living beings through spiritual beings and messengers. Love is the underlying guiding force of all of the universes, but its effect on living beings is seldom direct.

Love created all the universes and Thought is thus its creation as well.

 Thought is the fundamental force of Life.

Thought communicates with Love. Love allows an infinity within Thought because Love itself is infinite in its scope. It is essentially freedom of decision within Thought that has allowed Life to reproduce and to continue in its existence.

Humans are intensely complex beings. Much is given to us in Thought or by way of Thought. Aatnan made it very clear that much is expected of human beings in terms of the communication of Thought. What we think of as our own thoughts are really an accumulation of eons upon eons of thoughts held in our bodies and the unconscious mind of each of us. We can never know the full depth or the complexities of the interaction of our own thought with Thought. This includes not only the communication within our own human species but also the Thought that we share and communicate with all of Life.

Truly, the way to make sense of this Thought field is to feel one's way through it. To do this effectively, one must exercise Compassion. Compassion is that which allows the feelings, which are beyond direct communication, to be absorbed and, in some way, assimilated and, thereby, understood. The term "understanding" that we use is one that is limited to basically logical thinking, limited and circumscribed by language.

 Compassion requires suspending logical thinking.

We humans are always absorbing the thoughts of others without knowing it, without connecting to it, and without any sort of critical interpretation of any kind. Compassion involves using the senses in whatever ways appear appropriate to connect and focus on one's own feelings and on the feelings of the other.

Compassion is the Lesson that follows Calmness for the reason that Compassion cannot be done effectively without the ability to calmly reflect on one's own thoughts and feelings. Communication with another cannot be effective when one is being turbulently thrown about in one's own River. One's own River always includes, to some extent, the thoughts of others, through the Thought field that connects all humans, and all of life. Aatnan made it clear that all thoughts and feelings that one has are one's own responsibility, no matter where they have come from.

Spiritual growth requires calm appraisal and calm understanding with as much vantage and perspective that one can get of one's own River of Nows. Calmness allows one the opportunity to focus and intentionally connect with the thoughts of another.

> Compassion is never possible without Calmness, and it is never possible without intent.

In other words, one must want the connection and one must be willing to look at one's own River in a way that calms the River and all the many disparate influences that make focus difficult.

Compassion is necessary because it is essential to our own spiritual development and spiritual advancement. Only through Compassion is one able to approach the point of Now with some degree of awareness. It is at the point of Now that all influences of any kind happen to the individual living being.

Love is present in that intense instant moment of Now and all the array of infinite resources and influences are focused at that point. Compassion is what literally allows one to absorb the thoughts of another in something of a critical and knowing fashion.

Aatnan told me that Compassion can happen, in many instances but not always, without great effort. For this, there must be Calmness and an intent or a desire to be aware of one's own feelings and the feelings of the other. Awareness of one's own feelings and awareness of the feelings of another are essential to a good love relationship, but they are just as essential in every other kind of relationship that one has with another living being.

Being "aware" essentially means being comfortable in confronting the feelings of another with one's own feelings.

Compassion allows one to include in one's own immediate sense of being those thoughts and feelings of another. In those especially turbulent and deep parts of one's River, the exercise of Compassion can be something that requires greater focus, greater attention, and greater effort. There may be many intersecting Rivers and layers upon layers of feelings to process. For those most difficult feelings, and the most difficult relationships, the process of the Lesson of Inclusion will be essential to finding the part of one's self that must be accessed and reincorporated to effectively exercise Compassion.

The Lesson of Compassion teaches that being effective in one's own River requires an awareness of one's own thoughts and feelings. This works together with an awareness of how those thoughts and feelings are being affected in the combination of the thoughts with another. The effective exercise of Compassion achieves, at an elementary level, the act of Inclusion. This happens as Compassion gathers and contains one's own feelings while acknowledging, if not embracing, the feelings of the other.

The act of Inclusion results in our own feelings and those of others being included in a place of *advanced observation and enhanced perception.*

In the exercise of Compassion, Inclusion is often achieved without specific intention to do so. The Lesson of Inclusion teaches how to achieve it with specific intention. Spiritual growth—and all personal growth, while inevitably involving others—is fundamentally solitary in nature and must be done alone. To further one's own development, and to fulfill responsibility, sometimes one must help others and even bring them along one's path, at least for a time. This is especially true for family and loved ones.

The spiritual path that Aatnan spoke to me about is one that leads to a door that lets one person in at a time. The person at the doorway when I arrive will be me; and the one at the doorway when you arrive will be you. The Lesson of Inclusion teaches the re-incorporation within yourself of all the parts of yourself. Any part of you that is left isolated cannot be brought to your heart's energy. It can never connect to Love, the Creator. Nor can it drink of the elixir of your own true and integrated self.

How is it possible to integrate these isolated parts? One must consider several things. The first is a recognition that there may be, at least practically speaking, a part of you that is not feeling connected. This requires an act of courage to see that there may be a troubled or troublesome aspect of yourself, which, for whatever reason, does not want to interact with you.

Some might think, "How can I be in different pieces unless I am crazy or possessed?" It is not mainstream theology or mainstream psychology to believe that such internal splintering can exist in an otherwise reasonably healthy person. But believe it, because it happens, again practically speaking, to nearly everyone.

Once that hurdle of acceptance is overcome, the next thing to be concerned about is how to recognize the part or parts that are isolated. The Lesson of Compassion is useful in this regard. In general, when the application of the Lesson of Gratitude is not successful in allowing you to feel comfortable with yourself in whatever turbulence in the River has troubled you, it should be a good signal that there is something in you that does not want to be consoled with the usual language and awareness that you are accustomed to using.

You will know that trying to understand yourself emotionally in the troubled place is not working when you feel those telltale signs of the sinking feeling in your stomach; the heart that hurts or feels heavy; the shoulders that slump more than usual; the throat that feels like something is stuck there; the forehead that feels like it was hit by something; or the head that feels it is carrying an extra weight. Then, you will know it is time to accept the fact that you have a part of you that is not communicating, a part that has been ignored, a part that has not been developed, a part that needs nourishment with your personal attention.

The act of recognition is simple, courageous and generous. Its use will bring a shift in your awareness.

Trust that the true act of recognition will bring a response from the part that has been set aside. It will elicit quite different responses depending upon how alienated, how deeply isolated and how angry is the part of you that has been set apart.

Inevitably, you will find that some essential things are missing for the parts of you to become integrated into your true self.

The missing component is dialogue. To set up that dialogue will require a common language. One part of you may want to express things more with emotion, or artistic expression, while the other either enjoys expressing, or feels forced to express, itself logically and very conventionally. The isolated part may want to cry out that it is not allowed to express itself in feelings of love, while the other parts or parts only want to be free of intrusive, and possibly overly sexual, feelings.

In a way, this part of the Lesson of Inclusion is like Compassion applied internally. One part of you needs to exercise Compassion with the other. All parts need to calmly, and with all the understanding possible, embrace that other part that is perhaps ready to come out of hiding. You may hear things, and realize things you were not ready to accept. It may take time to accept it. It may be that all you can do for a good length of time is simply acknowledge that the part has a right to exist, peacefully, with all of you. Something short of denial may be all that you can do. That is enough to start the process of Inclusion.

232

The next step is to determine what else is missing. It won't all be missing dialogue. There will be something, maybe many things, missing. It may be resources in your life that you have not found. It may be a teacher for the art you never learned. It may be the lover you never allowed yourself to find. It may be the muscles you never developed, or the part of your mind that you ignored. It may be the books you never read. It may be the love you never found from your father, your mother, or others close to you. It may be money you never had, or feelings of importance that were denied to you. It will be some—or many—things that were not yours to enjoy or command. It will likely be complicated beyond your power of analysis to unravel.

Aatnan taught that, in this situation, there is one place to go. It is the Realm of Gratitude to which you must return.

You must go back to the moment of Now and find what there is in your world that has resources to give you what is missing. That instant moment of Now is where your Creator, Love, is providing whatever you are most intensely desiring. If you are desiring many and perhaps conflicting things, Love may be constrained to disregard them all, and give you nothing of what you desire.

Love will likely only give you what you most congruently desire.

Even then it may only give it to you when other things in your life and your universe coalesce to allow it to come into existence. It may take time, further attention, and further congruent intention and desire. Truly, nothing will come except through Love's provisions, from the infinite sources of the moment of Now.

Aatnan revealed to me even though Inclusion is an act about one's self, it is an essential act in the spiritual quest that he revealed. This lesson is necessary to give an unimpeded view of one's world by eliminating, part by part, those impediments to knowing one's self. Spiritual advance is all about acquiring the ability to observe and thereby becoming more and more like Love itself.

As Aatnan has said,

Love is the great force of pure observation.

Inclusion is an essential step that each individual human must make to advance one's own abilities of observation. Overcoming the most intense obstacles in one's self-discovery will lead to even greater advancements in the ability to observe both one's self and all the living beings that we encounter. Inclusion is ultimately about absorbing, and linking to, as much of the Thought of all living beings as can be done both consciously and unconsciously.

Aatnan told me that there are many other quests that have revealed ways to attain that level. The spirit's way is one of process and progress. It is one that is done by one's self, in the Realm of Gratitude, in connection with and by the assistance of Love, the Creator.

39

Acceptance as Inclusion

Aatnan then told me that he was leaving, not to return—at least for a while. One of the last dialogues I had with him before he left was about the fourth Lesson, of Inclusion.

He said that Love does not operate on the same level that we as living beings do. The observations of Love are far more intense and developed than anything our thoughts can conceive. Love connects with us through a desire to absorb and influence Life. Aatnan also said that Love uses messengers of Thought to connect with living beings. This connection is with and through Thought that is always present with all living beings. Love, itself, created and stays connected to Thought.

I asked Aatnan if we humans, in our development of our consciousness, and in our connection with the points of Now where Love connects with us, can request that Love give us specific thoughts, or specific information, or show us direction.

Yes, you can and, yes, you should.

The next question I had before he departed was whether, in our search for influences or in our development, we should seek to unite, as much as we possibly can, with all of Life and with all of Thought.

You should not confuse your existence with your River of Nows. That is certainly your life, and it is certainly something that you should always seek to understand, because that is the Realm of Gratitude in which you were born and in which you must remain until the end of your earthly existence. You can think of your River, to some extent, as the artifacts of your life, but not the energy of your life, and certainly not that which will develop your life or complete your life.

Much of the reason for the perpetuation of your River and your sense of continuity lies within

238

the rules of Wisdom, which, together with the force of Love, dictate the continuity of the physical universes.

What comes to you new, and allows you to be developed and to progress, is always mediated by Love, through the points of Now.

There is an infinity of available universes for each human.

What you find, when you find it, and how you accept it depends upon your intentions. Your River will have a tendency to always attract more of the same that it has had, in its intentions. This is merely the nature of the River and a tendency that it has to always attract more of the same that it has had. The mere fact of your earthly existence means that you will always, to some extent, be stuck in this conundrum.

To be free, to any extent, to bring in the untested, the unknown, or the foreign means that you must quiet the River and try to allow new intentions and new influences to be attracted to your River. It also means that you must seek to bring your intentions that are the most open and the most grand to your point of Now, to seek the attraction of other influences that can help to augment those intentions. It literally means to be as open, as open minded, as open of heart, and as free as you can be in the point of Now; to be a magnet attracting that which will complete you.

And so I have learned Love seeks to fulfill. It cannot do so until you begin a process of self-acceptance together with a sense of awareness of your own River and of the universe in which you are experiencing that River.

 Acceptance does not have to mean self-limitation. Nor does it have to mean that you are forever to repeat the same mistakes, or even the same actions.

Acceptance merely means that you recognize the fact of your River. This means accepting, at any given moment, the limitations and the grand possibilities of your River. It also means accepting the sometimes dangerous influences of the turbulence of your River.

The River is always the sum total of you and the other Rivers with which it has connected. Although you will not want to be lost in the turbulence of the River, some of the energy of the River and some of the influences of the River will be essential to building your complete and true self.

You must experience this energy and these influences to find out who it is that you must be accepting.

Inclusion means accepting the parts of your self and being aware, as much as possible, of the intention of each part. Inclusion always means taking that intention, or allowing the intention to be taken, to the heart. Carrying the intention to the heart brings a connection, through the moment of Now, to Love, the great Creator.

The fact of self-acceptance, of anything of even a minor nature, when coupled with a connection to Love and the point of Now, allows you the possibility of spiritual advancement.

Self-acceptance is another way of saying that a marginalized or excluded part of your self has been integrated by accepting the intention of that part. The heart feels without our mind knowing it. The mind assists the heart if the mind gives concurrent support for the connection, but that is not essential.

It is essential that you feel the intention as fully as possible. It is the heart that gives embodiment and substance to the intention. The stronger the heart feeling the more likely you are to find the connection with Love at the moment of Now.

The heart connection to the moment of Now, and the connection to Love, the Creator, is essential to achieve advancement with the four Lessons. Meditate on that. Feel it as strongly as you can. Gather your true intentions to that point, and you will be led to a connection and an understanding of Love and Wisdom.

40
The Benefits of
Using the Negative

was advised to pay attention to the negative by Aatnan. There is a lesson there of a useful purpose that should not be immediately rejected. The negative involves a lesson of something that is in need of fulfillment or in need of completion. It is part of the circle that needs to be closed. It needs the addition to the conscious awareness of something yet unknown.

We often think the negative is something that needs to be immediately uprooted and destroyed. We feel it does nothing except cause unhappiness, stunt, or destroy growth.

The negative nags at our deepest emotions. It is often well seated in both the conscious and unconscious minds. It engenders feelings that are uncomfortable. It is a loop constantly returning to the same feelings of inadequacy and belittlement. It is the place of shame. It is the place where things are hidden and it is the stuff of things denied.

The negative causes us to feel isolated and proves by the depths of its feeling why we need to be separated from others, even those close and loved by us. It is like an evil child that we would like to kill but cannot because of both the moral opprobrium and the sheer unthinkability of it. It would seem that deep in the heart of all of us who have negative thoughts and feelings is the knowledge that such thoughts are too important and too valuable to be tossed out like the morning newspaper.

In the end, we hang on to them. We nurture them. We let them grow even as we feel dragged down by them. It is because we know by instinct that there is something there that needs our attention and begs to be incorporated into the totality that we know we are.

Aatnan showed me the utility of the negative. I had not realized that it is a resource of sorts on its own. Negative thoughts, feelings and actions are the stuck patterns that we cannot escape. We are to cherish them as part of ourselves. They are a resource that the attitude of Gratitude would have us embrace.

The attitude of Gratitude requires that we seek the completion of the negative. It demands that we find the complementary part that fits the template of the negative and gives it completion. The complementary part shows how the negative is part of a whole that is no longer sad; or at least no longer sad only, but is part of something that has both a beginning and an end while not ending at all. It is the coat of many colors and the song that repeats its beautiful melody, never ceasing to uplift by its tune.

In a very brief flash, Aatnan told me that the negative, with all the feelings and thoughts it can bring forth, is to be deeply and fully embraced. From that full dose of the negative can we find its mirror in the future? The future brings the resources that prove what the negative was seeking. This will come to us by a projection into the future.

The future is only the immediate provision of resources at any instant moment of Now. It enters the River, adding to what the River already contains and moving always with the addition of new moments of Now. When the negative is given legitimacy, as if it has something to ask for, some way to lead you, it can be presented to the instant moment of Now in a way that requests those resources that will serve to complete the negative, changing it into a positive.

The positive is achieved in the way of resources that do not allow the negative to stay isolated.

When you practice this use of the negative, you will see how many resources, both internal and external come your way to give you some fulfillment. Doing so will not necessarily eliminate that negative thing you are seeking to avoid. That same negative may need to stay around longer to continue showing you parts of yourself that are in need of completion or fulfillment. Each use of the negative in this way will give you renewed strength of sense of purpose.

41
Application of the Lesson of Inclusion

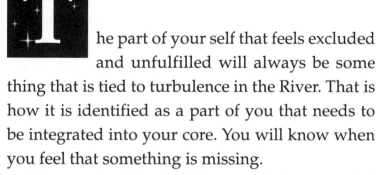

The part of your self that feels excluded and unfulfilled will always be some thing that is tied to turbulence in the River. That is how it is identified as a part of you that needs to be integrated into your core. You will know when you feel that something is missing.

You may feel deprived or ignored. You may feel that others do not appreciate you or do not care about your needs. You may, for instance, find yourself continuing to give to others in hopes that they will feel it in their kindness, or perhaps their debt, to give you what you need.

It is likely that as long as there is the turbulence in the River, you will not be able to achieve the inclusion of the isolated part, even if you are able some of the time to receive what the isolated part appears to want. Even if sometimes you feel that you are being supported and nurtured, when the reinforcement of the events of nurturing stop, or even slow down, you may well revert to the same feeling of deprivation.

The feeling of deprivation, of having something missing, will always have a connection back to the turbulence of the River. The turbulence of the River, once awakened, can easily resume its full torrent with only a little encouragement. The mind will always be connected to the turbulence and will be only too happy to give its logical justification for continuing the turbulence.

Turbulence in the River, with all of its emotional confusion and upset, always brings with it a concomitant mental confusion. The mind will respond to the turbulence with an overabundance of logical justification of why the isolated part must continue in its feelings of exclusion and isolation. It may be that the isolated part perceives a lack of a necessity. It may be that the isolated part communicates that it needs or deserves gratification that is not forthcoming.

Whatever it communicates as to the reason for the feeling of essentially being left out, there remains the fact that a looping behavior, seeking the same thing over and over, is causing the isolated part to remain separate and apart.

The isolated part engages in looping behavior by saying, in effect, "I don't get what I want, or need, so I have to stay out here more or less by myself," and it also says, "I am out here, more or less by myself, because I don't get what I want, or need." What it does not realize is that the only way to be reabsorbed and included is to stop the mental justification that the emotional turmoil is a reason to stay excluded.

The emotional turmoil is real. It makes its presence known throughout the body and beyond. Telling it to go away is fruitless. Trying to coax it away is, likewise, fruitless. Trying to talk it away will likely never fully succeed. It will come back even if it seems to go away for a time. Understanding the origins of the emotional turmoil of your life history may well help to minimize it, but won't likely eliminate it. Exercising Compassion for the isolated part, and for your whole self, is an essential prerequisite to exercising Inclusion.

 Full Compassion, without judgment, is what is required.

It may take time to achieve that Compassion. The calm and dispassionate understanding of the isolated part may take many sessions and some time. Compassion requires feeling the feelings as fully as possible. It also requires acknowledging that the feelings are supported by sufficient justification and are acceptable.

Compassion is an essential step to the Lesson of Inclusion. Compassion helps tremendously with the turbulence of the River, but it seldom can eliminate the turbulence. It is also not likely, by itself, to cause the isolated part associated with that turbulence to be reunited with your core.

 Reintegrating the isolated parts of yourself requires understanding of their intention.

Compassion will help provide you with understanding of those events and feelings in your life to which the turbulence is connected. For instance, the turbulence may be connected to a desire that you had at certain times of your life. That desire may have been to have the attention and love of your parent or guardian. It may have been a desire to have the connection and friendship of someone you knew. Or it may have been the desire for an amorous connection with someone in your life, and so on.

If that desire was met, at some time, with rejection, or, even worse, with abuse, psychological or physical, that would likely have been the perfect upset to have started a turbulence in the River of Nows. That turbulence may be strong enough and deep enough to continue life-long. That is the nature of the River.

All humans are perfectly wired to keep the turbulence swirling. Compassion for yourself, as you are related to that turbulence, will give you the basis for understanding that the events giving rise to the turbulence were real and serious. You will be given the ability to feel the feelings without the rejection of shame or moral judgment. You must come to understand that the feelings were, and are, very appropriate for what you endured.

The hurt that the little child felt when abused was very real, for instance. The hurt that you may have felt in being rejected, in some way, by your friends or classmates, was very real and you were well justified in feeling as you did. Even recalling the memory of it is understandably painful.

Everyone's River has turbulent places. For some the turbulence is very deep and accessed only on occasion. For others, the turbulence is more intense and more often encountered. The relative violence of the turbulence will vary with the person, but the effect of isolating a part of that person will never vary. It will always serve to keep the person fractured into parts that are, for one reason or another, felt unacceptable in one's core.

Compassion will give whatever knowledge you can find as to the connections and origins of the turbulence and it will let you know why your many feelings about it are justified. That is not the final step in being whole. Reuniting the whole person, in any sense, including the spiritual sense, is not just a mental exercise. A mere mental understanding will always fail.

 Mental understanding will fail for at least one fundamental reason: the mind is always the servant of perpetuating the turbulence.

It will always eventually take you back to the mental justification for the perpetuation of the turbulence. Using the example of the abused child, although the one who has been abused may be brought to an understanding of what was involved, and how the feelings are so real and justified, the next time there is something resembling, or reminding of, the abuse, the turbulence will likely be remembered and reawakened. The mind will give you all the old mental justification for retreating, hiding, and feeling ashamed.

Something more is needed to get out of the turbulence and to stay away from it for as much and as long as you can, perhaps forever.

Inclusion is needed. That requires accessing the infinite resources of the universes to find all the wondrous things that will satisfy the intention of the isolated part. That access always requires the assistance of Love, the Creator.

Compassion will give the understanding and the feeling that you will need to work with the isolated part in the Lesson of Inclusion. In the Lesson of Inclusion finding the intention of the part is what you will have to do. The intention of the isolated part has been to find something, be something, feel something that it has not, for whatever reasons, been able to accomplish.

In looking back on my experience and applying the Lesson of Inclusion, I saw that a large isolated part of myself has been the part that I have always felt did not get enough attention and gratification from lovers or friends. Based, as it has been, on a feeling of inadequacy of masculinity and worthiness, I would always take any instance of even slight rejection to justify the feeling of isolation and the basic need to separate to protect myself. I would tell myself, as advisors often urged, that I am perfectly in need and worthy of the love and attention of others.

I would, however, always find myself retreating into isolation, and from there, I learned from Aatnan, retreating into the turbulence of the River. Often, the slightest provocation would cause this retreat. For reasons always curious to me, the turbulence of the River provides a sense of safety that contemplating the unknown does not provide.

I felt that I had understood the intention of the part of me that felt inadequate and insufficiently loved. With some intensity, I had taken the desires and the intentions of that part to Love, the Creator. After leaving it there, out of habit I let my mind, with its internal voice, continue to chatter its old assumptions, jumping to the same old conclusions. Again, I allowed myself to retreat to the turbulence of the River.

While I was indulging in the turbulence of that old part of the River, the answer came to me, one day, loud and clear. I felt that my best friend had let me down and, using old assumptions and jumping to old conclusions, I frantically and furiously confronted him with the conclusion that he had let me down. I did the same with my wife. In both situations, the response I received was loving and embracing. Neither one took the occasion to respond in kind. My universe had fundamentally changed to accommodate the intentions of my isolated part.

Love, the Creator, had given me what I needed and showed that it was there. My mind had not yet comprehended that it had happened. I had failed in the essential application of faith and trust. I had not fully applied the fundamental rule of the Lesson of Inclusion, that the intention of the isolated part is all that matters.

And so, give that intention over to Love, the Creator, and don't make any assumptions of what you encounter.

> **Always expect that Love will be totally, completely, and miraculously fulfilled.**

Feel it with the entirety of your being. Hear it with the most beautiful music you know. Feel it with the most intense joy you can muster. See it with the vivid colors of the most incredible sunset you can imagine. Know that it is yours. I neglected to do that and I not only caused suffering to myself, but I caused suffering to others. Although suffering is the purpose of the turbulence of the River, Inclusion and Love do not embrace it. Love will feed your suffering when you place it in the instant moment of Now. Inclusion never wants it. Your higher nature of integration and increased perception never want it.

Finding and staying in touch with your intentions and your desires is by far the most important way to connect to Love, the Creator. It is also the most important way to achieve what you intend and what you desire.

42

The Spirit's Last Message

On December 27, 2007, I had one of my last conversations with Aatnan. I was told that he would not be in this part of the universe for some time. He would return, but not in time to help me finish writing out the last of the Lessons and the Truths he had taught me. He told me to continue to use my own words.

In that last meeting I had one more question: How can one find those parts within one's self that need to go through the process of Inclusion?

Aatnan told me not to forget the first three Lessons. He reminded me that all is in the Realm of Gratitude, in the River, and that anything disquieting in the turbulence of the River should first be taken into perspective by Calmness. He urged me to apply

Compassion to any part of me that was isolated or absorbed from someone else. Aatnan urged me to find and incorporate all those parts that feel separate.

If there is a comforting feeling that all is calm and satisfied, then Inclusion may well have taken place without needing anything from outside one's self. Any issues that remain disquieting then need to be brought to Love. I use the word disquieting, but that is not the word Aatnan used. He did not use any one word, but made it clear that anything that seems incomplete, in need of more development, or more work, or more of *anything* to reach a state of fullness, is something that needs work through Inclusion.

Again, he reminded me to be aware of those parts of my life, at home, at work or in my personal life that are in a state of process or development, waiting to reach a goal or some sort of conclusion. Those parts should be considered for the Lesson of Inclusion.

He showed me that the intent of the disquieted or incomplete part may not be clear. Aatnan said that in some situations it is the lack of clear intent that gives the disquieting feeling to the problem issue. He said that if the intent can be clearly stated, take that intent and give it to Love in the point of Now. Let the energy of the point of Now take the intent and find on its own what is needed from the infinite array of possibilities in the point of Now. It is best not to push this or to state preferences. If there is no clear intent, then simply take the feeling or the disquieting thoughts into the point of Now and let it be blended with the power of Love.

Something will come that will allow for Inclusion. It may not, and frequently will not, take the issue away from one's focus. It may be something that will need prolonged attention, and many connections with the point of Now to be resolved, or at least to feel resolved. The more open one is, and the more accepting one is of both one's own self and one's own worthiness, the more likely it is that some influences from the point of Now will have a clear and rapid impact.

Aatnan told me there is a great and immediate benefit to giving one's problem issues over to the power of Love. This takes the issue out of the cloak of repression. It has the immediate effect of letting one know that everything is or will be acceptable and workable. This can defuse the rumination, the anxiety, and sometimes the obsession that comes from issues that do not resolve or move along in the process of either growth or conclusion.

Finally, I asked of Aatnan, "How can one use Inclusion to process the absorption of others and, perhaps, eventually all of Life into one's River of

Nows?" He reminded me that what makes for Life is Thought. Thought surrounds us and is incorporated in us in ways that are either infinite, or virtually so.

 We all need to be open to the fact that our thoughts are not just our own, but a fantastically complex mixture of thoughts from all of Life.

The point of Now is one place to allow Thought to be mixed with our own intentions.

There are other times and events for incorporating thoughts into our own beings. He reminded me that there are messengers from Love that use Thought to connect us to Love and to the Thought field. He asked me not to forget that Compassion is important to be used in incorporating Thought outside ourselves. There is worthiness and meaning outside of ourselves. Merely acknowledging that opens us up, allowing us to grow and develop.

I was told:

Be ready to receive.

Before he left, Aatnan told me that there was still more to say to complete many of the messages he gave me. He told me that he was leaving me to do that, as he would not be here to provide input. He told me that he trusted I would be able to continue his Lessons. I did not get a chance to ask if there are other lessons beyond what he showed me. I imagine that there always will be Lessons.

After he was gone, there was a deep feeling of quiet. I felt the need to put his Lessons together so that others could hear them.

Epilogue

I t has been more than a year since Aatnan and I conversed but I continue the path he showed to me. I believe for all of us this journey to spiritual enlightenment is a process. It will take time and patience, and occasional steps backward. It is a process of constant unfolding of ourselves and an eventual connection of all of life to itself and to the Creator. Sometimes the road is easy, and sometimes it has bumps, but always it is leading us toward deeper awareness and observation that mirrors the divine. We are learning to restore our birthright.

At first when I heard Aatnan speak of "birthright," I thought it applied only to me. I now realize that it speaks of birthright of all of life, something we miraculously received and have passed down from eon to eon, ancestor to progeny, always miraculous and always touched by the divine.

The most primitive living cell divides itself without forethought of its own. The thought for that action is stored within the cell. The animals of the wild don't stop to think before reproducing and delivering their newborn to the wildness in which they live. The wild ones breathe free and easy. They move, stand and run with a knowledge we call instinct. The thought is programmed from something learned eons ago.

The smallest fish and the largest mammals of the oceans move in their world without asking for permission. The eagle, the condor and the tiny sparrow fly without any license at all. The bear needs no permission to hibernate. The spider weaves its intricate web of fabric stronger than steel, never stopping to consider who it needs to consult for that action. The same is true of the bacteria and the single cell organisms that inhabit our worlds.

Every living creature freely uses the Realm of Gratitude to the extent of its ability to observe it and to interact with it. As humans, due to our very high level of observation, ability to interact and manipulate our world, we have achieved a level of entitlement to the Realm of Gratitude that has been unknown to any other species of life.

A young man finds his lover as the expression of his heart, as the realization of his desire. Enfolded with that lover he fulfills a destiny of a race sprung from a desire from long, long ago. Connected heart to heart, the lovers observe themselves with an intensity that surpasses the five senses. They perceive themselves from vantage points that only the angels would know. They produce from their enfoldment an embodied expression of their own desires with thoughts of profound complexity.

Entitled to experience the full Realm of Gratitude, to experience the unbounded field of Thought, the young one feels the power of his own exuberance. Love provides in ways that are beyond understanding. This is the birthright, bounded in each instance of physical existence only by the rules of Wisdom, opened to the universe through Thought only by the limits of that universe.

The two lovers, in perfect love, find the Realm of Gratitude opened fully to them. Guided by their hearts, their desires are fulfilled in the abundance that they find and that they create. Perfect is their entitlement. Blessed by their connections to the infinite Universes they find their sustenance and their treasures given to them freely by Love. Such gifts Love gives to the ones connected so fully to the Realm of Gratitude.

The Realm of Gratitude, however, does not ensure perfection, only abundance, only infinite possibilities, recognized or not. Paradise is found in that infinite abundance, as are tragedy and broken hearts. At times paradise is merely a glance away from tragedy, or a few moments away from the broken heart. Such are the infinite possibilities of the Realm of Gratitude.

Think of the young father working at his job, rearing his children, each day presenting a new challenge. Some days bring great obstacles, others none. His mate may support him one day, and not another. So many days are repeated doing the same thing over and over in what seems like an endless, thankless task. Opposition surfaces, difficulty, and sometimes cruelty. He stays with what he is doing, with his intent so clearly stated in his daily struggle in the face of the difficulties of the day. His heart burns with many desires, some easily expressed and others not.

Asked on some days, he might tell you that his life seems to be a failure; focusing on the lack of perfection in his busy and complicated life. Abundance may be hard to see amidst the chaos. His mind is filled with his intentions, and his heart burns with his desires. Those intentions and desires are being met by his Creator. Never is the connection lost, though he may fail to see this in the immediacy of his labors. Entitled he may well not feel, yet entitled he is.

Is he without hope? No matter the enormity of his travails or impediments, can he not find his way?

Or, consider a young girl whose life was spent in isolation and apparent misery. She was lost and disconnected not only from others, but also from herself. She could think—in fact, she was quite brilliant—but that fact was unrecognized by others when she was young. She could taste and she could feel. But her behavior at the table and around others lacked any hint of skill.

The abundance of the Realm of Gratitude was revealed when she was allowed to connect to the world through the efforts of a wonderful and dedicated teacher. She learned to communicate; to use her feelings to substitute for other senses lost; and to experience seemingly all that the world had to offer her. She became one of the best-known, highly regarded and celebrated individuals of her day, dining with princes and presidents. Her only drawback was that she was deaf, blind and dumb. Her name? Helen Keller.

Helen Keller proved the grand extent of her birthright even though she was bound by limitations that most of us would find totally disabling. She would likely have said that what she was allowed to do could be done by nearly anyone.

It is there for all; and all do it to some extent. It is there for the asking, in the Realm of Gratitude. It is in the asking, it is in the doing, and it is in the taking. Be careful what you ask for, you may get it. When it is laid before you, take it and use it to the best of your abilities. When in doubt, do something, even if you think it may be wrong. To live in the Realm of Gratitude without exploring its possibilities is to live only part of your life. Explore it as if it is your birthright. It is.

When times are poor, everything seems limited. And when times are rich, everything seems unlimited. All are the Realm of Gratitude in different phases. As the old saying goes, Rome was not built in a day. The passages of life are dictated in our genes, from infancy through old age. All are governed by the rules of Wisdom.

We filter the Realm of Wisdom through these dictated formats, and through them, we exercise our own powers of observation. The filters may be limited and the process may be constrained in terms of speed, but the promise of unlimited possibilities remains. Step-by-step, one foot up and one foot down, that is how the possible becomes actual. It is in the stepping that we experience the road. It is in experiencing the road that we know the extent of the Realm of Gratitude. In the brevity of our lives we cannot experience everything, nor does any one person see life the same as does another. Yet within these apparent limitations we are given access to the infinite, mediated through the beneficence of our Creator.

To achieve the promise of our birthright and bringing it into our reality requires action and commitment. Large parts of the Realm of Gratitude can be experienced without conscious thought, but others require involvement and discernment. Most of all, you must open your heart to yourself. Doing so requires inclusion of as much of yourself as you can find, and then it requires inclusion of as much of life as you can.

As Aatnan points out, when one is tumbling in the turbulence of the River, access to the benefits of the Realm of Gratitude can be disrupted. Getting out of the turbulence and back into your full self and capable of enjoying your birthright, requires passing, however slowly or quickly, through the steps of the lessons of Aatnan.

The interruption of the Realm of Gratitude can be demonstrated by a young man who was bedeviled by hard feelings, if not hatred, for his stepfather who had abused him severely as a child.

He tumbled in this place in his River, drowning in his hatred and self-hatred and frequent feelings of failure. He nearly went under in his River and thought often that it would be easier just to end his existence. Far from feeling entitled to any birthright, he called himself a "virus" and felt that he did not deserve to enjoy the unlimited benefits of his Realm of Gratitude.

He was given the four Lessons of Gratitude, Calmness, Compassion and Inclusion. Each became a stepping stone, calmly allowing him to view his dilemma and have compassion for himself in relation to his stepfather. He tempered his ill feelings toward his stepfather and discovered he had empathy for him. Through a process of Inclusion, he was able to find a part of himself that he had allowed to be set aside by the turbulence of his River.

Shortly after finding this part of himself, his stepfather called upon him in a time of grave need and a miracle of reconnection happened. His reconnection to himself led directly to a reconnection to his stepfather and then to a reconnection to his own birthright. In turn, it led to recovering a sense of his own self-confidence, all of which furthered his ability to effectively deal with other challenges in his life. Dealing successfully with his own challenges then led him to grasp some magnificent opportunities that were available to him in the Realm of Gratitude.

This young man demonstrated how finding and re-including lost or alienated parts of one's self can reveal further possibilities and opportunities in life. It is one of Aatnan's lessons that only by connecting more fully with one's self can one connect with the rest of Life.

The birthright is a gift that originated with the creation that Love began and continues this instant. It stretches back to the beginning of the infinite universes, layered between the gifts of the Realm of Wisdom and connected through Thought to the very beginning of Life. Your own thoughts, as a part of the great field of Thought, directly affect what the Creator will manifest. What you manifest will be layered between the nearly infinite array of gifts that the Creator assists in bringing to you in every instant of every day of your life. This is the stuff of miracles.

Opening all the senses and observing well what is around you is the best way to start experiencing the fullness and the exultation of the Realm of Gratitude. You did not ask for it and you did not create it, yet it is your immense birthright to have been given an awesome ability, even a mandate, to co-create the universe that you are in at any given instant moment.

Until Aatnan told me what was in the Realm of Gratitude, I did not realize how much is, and was, possible with the resources available to each of us every day. I did not know how my own heart could leave messages to the Creator. Nor did I know the *exultation* that is available at any time by reaching back to that place in the heart where the River of Nows begins. I had taken the perceived limitations in my life as something fixed and certain. I did not know that personal achievement could be connected, as Aatnan taught, to my own spiritual development.

The messages of Aatnan made me realize that what one truly intends, and what one truly desires, in both physical and spiritual realms, will have the assistance of the Creator in bringing to reality.

If your life, your River of Nows, is always pleasant, accommodating, calm and acceptable, consider yourself blessed. You may have no need to intend or desire anything other than what you have. If, however, you are like the huge majority of the rest of us who find the turbulence overwhelming from time to time, you may need Aatnan's lessons to find your way back to your secure central core. Any area of turbulence in your life need not remain a recurring trap for you. Find your way out. Become the whole and full person that you are meant to be. Aatnan assures you that it is your birthright.

You are a divine creature. But then, so is the amoeba and maybe even the virus, according to Aatnan. He perceives the divinity in all of life, being the ability to mimic the Creator's own immense power of observation. It has been said many times in different ways that Life is a reflection of the divine Creator.

Aatnan's lessons provide a different take on that. You are divine because it is your heritage, from the inception of Life's existence, to resemble the essence of the Creator. His lessons provide a framework for understanding that.

Practicing the Lessons

Aatnan had been very clear in saying that no one reaches mastery in the Realm of Gratitude before also reaching enlightenment. In fact, for nearly all humans, the Realm of Gratitude becomes increasingly complex and convoluted as each moment of Now is added to the River. This comes in the form of new experiences, new faces, new relations, new words, and many, many more new things. All add to the amazing complexity of each life.

Aatnan further clarified that turbulence of the River can never be overcome without achieving some perspective of what is happening in the River. This perspective always involves taking a view that is removed in some way from that turbulence. That removal may be as simple as drawing a picture of what is in the turbulence or how it feels. It may be by seeing that turbulence as if from a distance. This can be done, for example, by imagining that you can see yourself and others from a distance of ten feet, two hundred feet, or more. It is in the place of Calmness that the perspective can be gained.

Practicing the Lesson of Calmness requires removal from the emotion of the River's turbulence. Being aware that there is turbulence is the first step in being able to address it with Calmness. When you are caught up in the turbulence of the River, thinking about how to see it in perspective is the last thing on your mind. Feelings of anger, fear, imminent danger, and other overwhelming feelings will grip every part of your mind and most of your body. The turbulence may give an advance warning that it is coming, but that is likely the rare event.

Usually, the turbulence starts before there is time to think much about it. Cutting it off before it gets completely overwhelming is usually about all that you can do.

Therefore, being able to know that you are in the place of turbulence is essential.

It may involve a feeling in the pit of the stomach.

It may involve hearing deflating or angry Self-talk.

It may be a tight feeling in one's throat or one's chest.

Not everyone feels it in the same place or in the same way. The Lesson of Calmness teaches that one must step aside and recognize that danger has arisen. In the rarest situation, it may also involve actual physical danger. Most likely, the danger is a mere figment of imagination. Unless you are in fear of danger to life or limb, the best that can be done is to step back and quietly wait until the turbulence has passed.

Even in a situation of great plenty and gratification, in the tumble of the turbulence peace, happiness, and tranquility will seem very far away. Calmness allows for perspective. Perspective allows for observation and understanding. Both are essential steps on the way to spiritual advancement—any advancement requires Compassion and Inclusion of all separate and isolated parts.

Love is always there, giving us what we need; we just don't know it. The isolated and wounded parts do not receive all the sustenance and resources they need for precisely the reason that they are left isolated and separate. Those parts are treated as if they have no right to be incorporated into the other parts that are flourishing with what they need.

The longer that they are isolated and treated as separate parts, the more likely it is that they will stay that way. The challenge is to take the isolated part and gently take it to that place where infinite resources are found.

Seldom is there a person who has only one issue with one part of himself or herself that is isolated and apart from his or her core. Most reasonably complex individuals have many such isolated or ignored parts. Encountering as many of them as possible is essential to spiritual growth using the path that Aatnan teaches.

Above all else, Aatnan wants you to know the turbulence is always a signal that it is you whom you are seeking to find. Every turbulent moment will involve some part of yourself that has been left alone. It will be a part that you, and perhaps others, have intentionally or unintentionally, pushed aside.

By the turbulence, you will know that the isolated part has not been respected. You will know that it has not been fed and has not been brought into the warmth of your center core. You must seek to find that part and embrace it even if you do not know exactly what it needs, specifically, to feel fulfilled. Take it to the Creator and ask that the intent and desire be fulfilled.

Always know that you can take the isolated part and bring it to the place where Love, the Creator, resides. Have the faith that all that is necessary will be provided for your sustenance and fulfillment. You will regain all the energy that you have ever put into worry by leaving your intent and your desire for fulfillment in the grasp of the immense energy of Love, the Creator.

The Lessons of Aatnan let you know that you are already on the road to spiritual advancement and spiritual mastery. Your success will depend upon how you deal with the turbulence of your River. Re-incorporating lost and isolated parts of yourself will bring you strength and understanding. You will be able to better enjoy yourself and those around you.

I wasn't ready for Aatnan to leave me when he did. I wanted him around me, to feel both the wisdom and comfort of his sage words. There is so much that Aatnan did not reveal.

He did not tell me how Love, the Creator, communicates with Life, or how we as humans can better communicate with Love.

He did not give me any instruction on understanding the process of the Realm of Wisdom.

He did not give me any detailed instruction on connecting with or communicating with the Thought field that Life creates.

So many questions were left. I do know that he left it to me and to others to follow the path of his Lessons.

Why should I have been chosen to transmit the spiritual teachings of a spirit from far away? How do I know and how do you know that I have not just imagined this series of Lessons?

Does that make a difference? Aatnan was real to me. The subject matter and the flow of the words was not what I had been accustomed to as a lawyer. I would not have felt comfortable speaking, nor writing, that way. If his Lessons only give you a pathway to understanding how you fit within yourself, and within this corner of the universe, it will have been worth the while in bringing them to you.

What Aatnan did leave me was a framework for putting myself on the spiritual path, and for sharing and teaching it to others. It is now my task, and the task of others impressed with Aatnan's words and Lessons, to provide practical ways to implement them. So much can be done to get us ready for a deeper connection to ourselves and to our Creator. I'm ready. Are you?

Afterword

As *Turbulence in the River* was in the final processes of editing, I again heard from Aatnan. In meditation, I had asked if Aatnan was near and I was surprised to hear him say in that calm, deliberate voice he had returned. This time, he had brought with him kindred Spirits to help with what they feel is a serious condition of life on this Earth. I knew I could use his help, and the others, in the follow up to his Lessons.

When Aatnan left me after dictating the Lessons and the two Truths, I had been thinking and meditating on Thought, the connections of Life and how to understand our mutual life purposes. On May 31, 2010, Aatnan gave me the following message:

Words we are beyond, and in the communication of thought it is the being and the heart that is of the essence. The Thought that we are looking for is beyond status, beyond appearance, beyond words, and certainly beyond common understanding. Thought becomes possible by the acceptance of the deep complexity of the realm of wisdom and its offspring, the living beings of the Universes. Thought is everywhere living beings are. It is in the beauty of your gardens and in the hells of your prisons. It is in war and it is in peace. It is in birth and it is in death. It is in the wonder and it in the horror.

You will miss so much of Thought if you wait for words to come to you that you already know. You will also waste your time with Thought if you only look for emotions you have known before. Thought was born looping around itself in the most primitive life that began. It continues to loop and twist around itself.

It has been only by leaps of rare insight that life has made changes that have added to its complexity and added to its ability to more deeply observe the universe around it. With the near infinite complexity of life on your planet in recent times, the rare insight is happening more often but is still not commonplace.

Deeper levels of spiritual development require becoming attuned to the rare insight. The rare insight that allows the Thought field to become more developed in its ability to observe, always has as its impulse the desire to correct dissonance in the communication/ interconnection between living beings.

Dissonance has been an integral part of life since its inception. Life shows its kinship with the Realm of Wisdom in its tendency to degrade and decay. It is found in anger, hatred, war and destruction. Death of the living being shows it at its most pronounced. Remember the expression "Blessed are the peace makers for they shall inherit the Earth," and in that you find an example of how to eliminate dissonance around you.

Look and listen for the dissonance in yourself and others around you. The four Lessons and knowledge of the two Truths will give you a method for resolving the dissonance in yourself. That is not enough to eliminate dissonance. You will continue with dissonance always because it is an integral part of Life that you will encounter among living beings. Seeing it

*in the world around you, how you perpetuate it
and encourage it yourself, and how those
groups and organizations that you are a part of
tend to create dissonance, may reveal a way
of dealing with the dissonance you encounter.*

*Look and listen for the dissonance around you,
and continue to use the four Lessons to attempt
to eliminate the dissonance or to minimize and
deal with the dissonance that you have in
yourself.*

*The dissonance in yourself you feel as
turbulence, and the dissonance that is around
you in the human life and the other living
beings on the planet is felt as something that
does not fit together, something that causes
always a method of destruction.*

As a follow up to his message, I would add: As you
work to remove or cope with the turbulence in
your Life, you will become increasingly aware of
the dissonance and the programmed destruction
that you see in the world around you.

In much of it, you will be constrained to participate either as a dance you cannot avoid, or as the

lesser of evils. You will tolerate certain dissonance because you must choose your battles well. The dissonance around you is most often not something personal to you. It is simply part of the tension of the tangled world around you.

Your goodwill and your desire to minimize the dissonance, and thereby the turbulence, of those around will serve to elevate the ability to observe, and thereby the spiritual development, of all.

—Michael G. Sawaya

Further Discussion of Key Terms and Concepts

The following are some of the key words and concepts used by Aatnan in the conversations I had with him. Many of these terms have meanings and significance beyond what we ordinarily understand them to mean.

Calmness

The Lesson of Calmness shows how to achieve clearer and less disturbed perception. Aatnan showed me a few ways to practice Calmness. There is no limit to the ways that one can practice and cultivate it. Calmness is always connected to the Realm of Gratitude. For that reason it cannot be separated or disconnected from the River, and especially not from the instant point of Now. That is the place where Love connects and where we access the infinite universes. Keeping that connection strong and vibrant is integral to each of the four Lessons.

Calmness, at least exercised intermittently, is what allows for the moments of insight that free us, at least for a while, from the River. It allows us to see connections in the River and in the parts of our selves which were not apparent before. It allows us to see the humor in our lives, allowing for many of the things that give humans their unique capacity to both rearrange and enjoy our world. Perhaps most importantly, it allows each human the moments of reflection to understand how each other individual life form relates to us through the events, connections, and turbulence of the River. Calmness allows for a sense of boundaries, giving us an understanding of our unique individuality. With Calmness, we see the ambiguity and the sometimes disjointed nature of the River.

In the last analysis, viewing the River with Calmness creates the opportunity for us to see that the River itself can be seen as an illusion, a figment of our memory. We begin to see that the River is in some ways a store of emotions felt and perhaps emotions to be felt. Calmness is an essential element to any process of understanding how each life form connects and relates to the physical world run by the rules and processes of Wisdom.

Aatnan showed that the physical world of Gratitude is where the action is. Nothing happens to achieve spiritual advancement except in that Realm. Any attempt to avoid the Realm and its intricacies is simply a trip through our mind that will lead only in a circle back to where we started.

Compassion

By seeing the River more clearly, and avoiding as much as possible its turbulence, we are able to see other life forms as distinct and integral in themselves. By being aware of other forms, we are able to approximate some understanding of at least parts of our River through the exercise of the Lesson of Compassion.

Before Compassion was revealed to me, I had thought that being compassionate was primarily to help another being, as an act of mercy or some other essentially paternal gesture. With Aatnan's guidance, I've learned that it is so much more. Essentially, the Lesson of Compassion advances the spirit by separating and legitimizing one's own separate parts and any others who are in the turbulent places in the River. What we typically think of as an act of compassion is actually an outcome while practicing the Lesson of Compassion. That act of compassion is not, however, the spiritual reason for living through Compassion.

Each part of our self, and others involved in our River, has a purpose and an emotional matrix that requires a minimal level of respect and recognition. The various parts of our self and others in our River intersect and affect each other. We must attempt to avoid being dependent upon others; by doing so, we make them dependent. The result will bind us, and them, to the turbulence of the River.

 Separating from the turbulence of the River is the principal purpose of practicing the Lesson of Compassion.

Compassion is to some extent an art. It involves not just the logical parts of our brain, but all of our being, to sense the presence of others and the feelings, including nonlinear and non-logical aspects, of that other part or that other being. Recognizing and legitimizing a part of our self, or another, never diminishes the status of other parts or of other individuals.

Quarreling over feelings or aesthetic matters serves only to entangle us more deeply in the turbulence of the River. It is a spiritual impediment. The Lesson of Compassion has simple rules, but the practice involves all the complexity of the individual. It is a practice of a lifetime. Knowing how and when to use it can prevent the bashing one will get from the turbulent places in the River.

The Four Lessons: The Process

The practice of Inclusion requires going through the process of the first three Lessons. There are those who are very adept at working within the Realm of Gratitude. Many have achieved a fairly solid spiritual base by merely understanding their world well and enjoying the fruits of that world. Some will stay there and be perfectly happy and reasonably spiritually intact. Others have gone from the Realm of Gratitude and learned Calmness, staying at that level without feeling the need to cultivate the third Lesson, Compassion.

There is no universal law that anyone needs to proceed further. However, if there is dissonance, if there is a tendency to fall often into the turbulence of the River, and if Calmness does not provide sufficient solace, Compassion is essential to break away from the turbulence. From there, it will likely be necessary to proceed to finding and including the parts of one's self that have been unfulfilled, by using the processes of the Lesson of Inclusion.

Gratitude

Gratitude, the first lesson, concerns the real, physical world and provides the fundamental basis of the teachings imparted by Aatnan. Aatnan spent the most time with me transmitting the Lesson of Gratitude.

He proposed a new way of looking at our world, ourselves, our abilities, and, indeed, all the resources that are available to us in our lives.

 Aatnan taught me that the physical world that we live in has resources beyond our imagination, and he wanted me, and those hearing his Lessons, to know that we should never feel unduly limited in our thoughts of our own capabilities or our opportunities.

Unbelievable possibilities are opened to us:

It is in the Realm of Gratitude that we discover who we are; and it is in that Realm that Love, our Creator, connects with us, listens to our intentions and supports us in the direction that we take.

It is in the Realm of Gratitude that we are directed; and it is within that ground that we come into this world and leave this world.

It is in the Realm of Gratitude that we connect with the heart; find the moment of Now; experience what Aatnan told me was the River of Nows, and where we find the incredible energy in the place where the Now begins.

Learning how to connect and use that connection with the heart at the point of the moment of Now has proved to me to be essential to the spiritual development that the Lessons afford.

Inclusion

Before the meaning of the Lesson of Inclusion was revealed to me, I thought that the value of Inclusion must be to bring an understanding and meaning of others into each of our own lives. I was wrong; that is not what it means.

The act of Inclusion is to bring all parts of our self back to one's self. It is making all parts of the individual's being "available." This was revealed to me in a dream. As I shut my eyes one night, I had asked Aatnan to give me some understanding of how to explain Inclusion in this book. In my dream, I clearly heard his voice saying,

Make all of yourself available to yourself.

This means bringing any identifiable part of our self directly into the Now, and as close to the point of the moment of Now as is possible. All is to be brought, as an act of faith, to the moment of Now. No part of our self can be left separate. This does not happen without bringing to the point of Now the intention or intentions that the part is expressing, or seeking to express. Every aspect of our self seeking to find expression has an intention, expressed or unexpressed. When there is a part of our self that feels unattached, distant, estranged, uncomfortable, or in some way ill at ease with the rest of our self or our self-expression, there is something that it is seeking to accomplish. It may be something:

It wants to experience or something it wants to express;

It wants to have heard by one's own inner voice or perhaps said by someone else;

It wants to have been accepted by one's self or by others;

It may involve health, self-image, vocation, sex or love life.

Usually, it is something that has a goal unrealized, or some desire that has been ignored, suppressed or unfulfilled.

Bring that aspect to the point of Now, purposefully leaving it there. Love connects to the instant point of Now, allowing it to attract, even find, in the infinite possibilities of the instant moment of Now those influences, forces, or physical things that will fulfill or complete the intention of that aspect of our self.

Life

The word Life is used to signify all living beings; the spirit of all living beings; and the general process that created replicating beings.

The Now

Each Lesson has a practical part. Aatnan illuminated the realm of spirituality as an integral part of Life to be cultivated, processed and perfected in our daily life and in all things. It begins with being truly present.

With Aatnan's guidance, I learned that being present in the Now is essential to understanding our world.

The moment of Now is the infinitely small instant of time in which Love observes the universes, and at that instant, Love creates the infinite resources of the universes.

Observation

In revealing the Truth of Love, Aatnan showed me how the physical universe was the Creator, Love, observing itself. The infinite universes are kept intact through the continued observation of Love. Life partakes of the power of observation; it is a physical manifestation of Love's capacities of observation.

The first action of a simple molecule to reproduce itself involved an act of observation, and that act immediately attracted the attention and devotion of Love to the multiplying molecules. Everywhere molecules are reproducing, Love is present in rapt attention; attached, and absorbing energy from them.

Aatnan pointed out it was not a matter of importance whether the act of reproducing was specifically planned by Love, in advance, or whether it happened

as a random event. The *very first act* of Life's reproduction involved an act of Thought.

 Thought was that intangible but essential influence or force that made reproduction possible.

Love did not, and does not, direct each individual
thought. Rather, Love influences Thought by attaching itself to all acts of reproduction and absorbing the
Thought of that reproduction. With that absorption,
itself an act of observation, Love affects each action of
each molecule involved in the Life that supports the
act of reproduction. Love is present in each and every
Thought of each and every living entity.

Perception and Enlightenment

Perception is based on awareness and is essential to
the practice of the lessons of Calmness, Compassion
and Inclusion. The practice of advanced awareness
through the use of perception allows us to work
with the issues of turbulence in the River of Nows.
The result is that we can better achieve the benefits of
these three Lessons. Perception also has an essential
role in one's connection to the Creator. The replenishing of Love, the Creator, is increased with each

higher level of observation. For that reason Love, the Creator, encourages higher levels of perception.

In a manner of speaking, each level of perception (being more advanced observation) takes the individual life form closer to Love itself. At a certain advanced place of observation, it gets so close to the observation capacity of Love that it is absorbed into Love and ceases to exist in connection to the physical form. This is the ultimate of Enlightenment.

River of Now

Aatnan was very clear in his message—all spiritual development takes place in the physical universes, in the Realm of Gratitude. The River of Nows is the place in which all physical forms of Life exist. To some extent, it is an illusion of our senses that the infinite stream of Nows appears as a River. However, it is due to the rules and processes of Wisdom that we are allowed to know and feel the River. All memories, all emotions and all our neurological activity, in both brain and body, are bound to Wisdom's rules and processes. Do not ignore them.

No one can advance without being aware and attempting to understand them as much as possible. Dealing with the complexity within the River of Nows is a problem and opportunity, that each of us encounter. The River of Nows is inevitably turbulent and at times, violent. Understanding the River; being aware of what is going on; and discovering why, is an essential part of spiritual advancement.

As long we are kept captive by the turbulence of the River, we cannot achieve much perception at any level; we cannot achieve a perspective on what is happening in that spot or those spots of turbulence. Think of it as fighting to survive while being sucked into a whirlpool. It is common to us all, if we cannot look around to find our opportunities, we will stay stuck in one or more of the many turbulent places in our lives.

 All humans have turbulence in the River of Nows. It is an inevitable part of living.

Thought

The use of the word "Thought" is likely to be different than the usual use of it, and I have to confess, this particular word took me a bit of getting used to. Aatnan distinguished the term thought—those exchanges of information in the human brain—from Thought.

Human thought is part of the greater Thought and is, in fact, a refinement of Thought. Human thought is *all* the things that living beings do to transmit information.

The greater Thought is the sum total of all the processes that each part of living beings use to maintain themselves and to reproduce. According to Aatnan,

It is an immensely powerful force that attracts Love to it.

Thought expands to Thought Field and Thought and Love. Separate discussions on each follow.

Thought Field

Thought will endure only as long as Life endures. Individual thoughts endure for a short time only, but together, all individual thoughts coalesce into what we can think of as a Thought field. This field must extend far beyond the physical living entity.

Individual thoughts are more advanced in each level of perception that is achieved. We can think of this as looking upon looking.

Within each individual organism, there are highly complicated acts of observing the act of observation.

Each cell has actions that react to other actions, and there are mechanisms in place to regulate each reaction upon an action. Humans that use Thought to see, hear, or conceptualize the global or entire creation, and the community of those and other life forms, are evidencing an even more advanced and higher level of observation.

Thought and Love

Thought was revealed to be complex beyond imagination. Even the most rudimentary forms of Life involve Thought that is more complicated than a myriad of computers can possibly simulate and certainly more than can be fully explained. Thought is an influence or force that extends well beyond the specific locality of the individual molecules of Life.

Where the physical aspects of the molecules of Life are limited by the rules and processes that bind Wisdom together, Thought is not so limited. Thought can be present in one place and transmitted to or be also present in some other physical locality far distant. This is especially true of the complex thoughts of advanced life forms, and certainly true of human beings.

Thought was not essential to the creation of the universes. Only the act of Love's observation was required.

Love involves itself with Thought because Life fills each universe with this influence or force.

Love uses it to replenish its own store of that force, which assists it in its constant observation.

Love has messengers that communicate by Thought to individual life forms.

Love does not as a rule communicate directly, without messengers, to any individual life form.

The presence of Love is highly influential but usually not direct. There are innumerable spirits, messengers and guides that Love uses to communicate with Thought. None of them are limited by the rules and processes of the physical universes. They cannot be revealed or explained by the rules or processes of the physical universes. For that matter, Love also cannot be explained by those rules or processes.

Thought is similar to Love in its act of observation. Love endures, but Thought does not have that power of endurance. The power of the observation of Love is the constant of the universes, and it will continue to exist after the universes that we presently know are spent and exhausted. When, for whatever reason, Love either cannot or will not continue its act of constant observation, the physical universes will implode, instantly, to nothing.

The Truth of Love

Having been well steeped and well trained in many of the branches of Christianity; having read the Holy Bible three times cover to cover and many hundreds of times with various passages in both the Old and New Testaments (including reading the first four Chapters of the New Testament in Greek), I thought that I well knew what Love was. It was a surprise when Aatnan revealed the definition of this Truth to me. I was shown that Love is essentially the force of observation. He told me that Love created the universes by looking upon itself; and that the force of this power of observation is immense beyond imagination.

Not only did this force of observation create the universes, it has literally kept them intact, and growing, since creation. Love does this by continuing to observe each and every thing in those universes from the smallest to the largest units we can see or measure.

Once Love was described to me, it opened up a new way of understanding Gratitude. Our Realm of Gratitude is created anew each instant by the force of Love's observation. At the point of the instant of

Now, Love makes available the infinite possibilities that form the basis of both the infinity of universes and the continued expansion of those universes.

The Truth of Wisdom

When the Truth of Love was revealed to me, I was also told that the Truth of Wisdom began at the instant of creation and became the companion of Love. Wisdom is the sum total of all the rules and intricate processes of the physical universes that came about through Love's observation. It appears to us as the universes that we know through our senses. All possibilities that we as humans know are available to us as permitted by the constraints of the rules and processes of Wisdom.

 There are infinite universes because at any instant there are an infinite number of possibilities that Love's observation detects.

Aatnan showed me that Wisdom's nature is to perpetuate, in physical form, the infinite array of combinations chosen; and to continue with that combination for as long as it can be maintained (until it eventually dissipates and is gone).

Tony Hillerman

A PUBLIC LIFE

John Sobol

ECW PRESS

Copyright © ECW PRESS, 1994

CANADIAN CATALOGUING IN PUBLICATION DATA

Sobol, John, 1963–
Tony Hillerman : a public life

Includes bibliographical references.

ISBN 1-55022-214-7

1. Hillerman, Tony – Biography. 2. Novelists,
American – 20th century – Biography. 1. Title.

PS3558.145Z78 1994   813'.54   C94-932052-8

This book has been published with the assistance of the Ministry
of Culture, Tourism and Recreation of the Province of Ontario,
through funds provided by the Ontario Publishing Centre, and with
the assistance of grants from the Department of Canadian Heritage,
The Canada Council, and the Ontario Arts Council.

Design and imaging by ECW Type & Art, Oakville, Ontario.
Printed and bound by Imprimerie Gagné, Louiseville, Québec.

Distributed by General Distribution Services,
30 Lesmill Road, Toronto, Ontario M3B 2T6.
(416) 445-3333, (800) 387-0172 (Canada), FAX (416) 445-5967.

Distributed to the trade in the United States exclusively
by InBook, 140 Commerce Street, P.O. Box 120261,
East Haven, Connecticut, U.S.A. 06512.
Customer service: (800) 243-0138, FAX (800) 334-3892.

Distributed in the United Kingdom by Drake Marketing,
St. Fagans Road, Fairwater, Cardiff CF5 3AE, (0222) 560333.

Published by ECW PRESS,
2120 Queen Street East, Suite 200,
Toronto, Ontario M4E 1E2.